## About the Author

JOHN GILHOOLY worked for newspapers in reporting, editing and design capacities for more than 20 years. He owned a typesetting and design business for 10 years. Recently, he has been writing nonfiction and fiction.

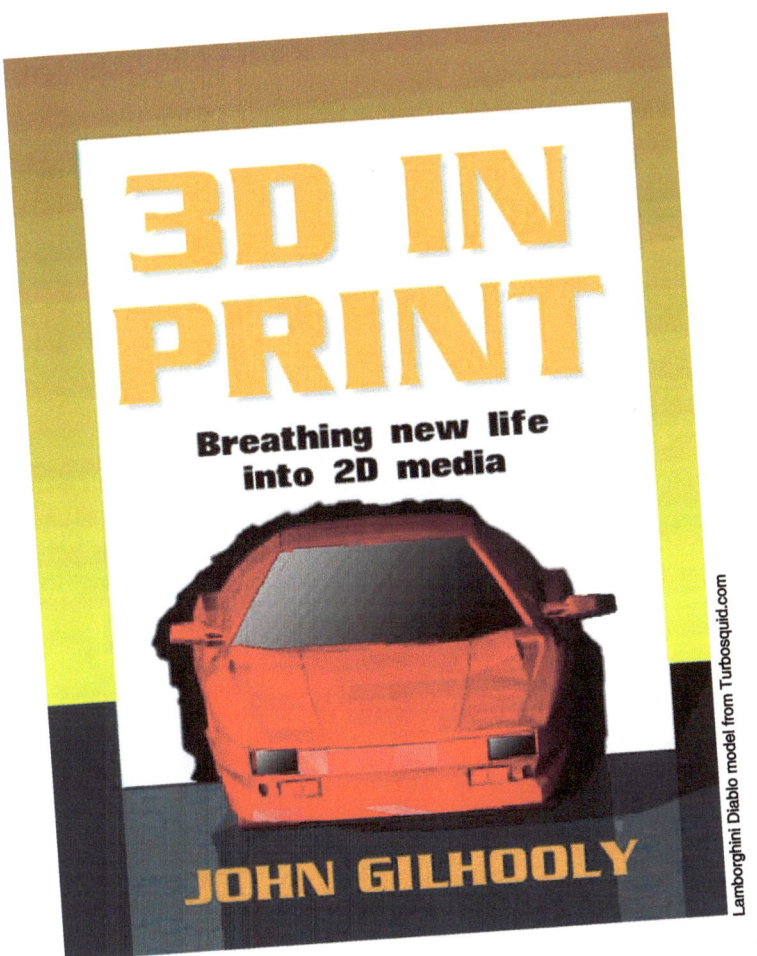

# 3D IN PRINT

**Breathing new life into 2D media**

## JOHN GILHOOLY

## McNeil & Richards

ISBN 13    978-0-9825602-3-5
ISBN       0-9825602-3-0

Published by McNeil & Richards
USA

# 3D in Print

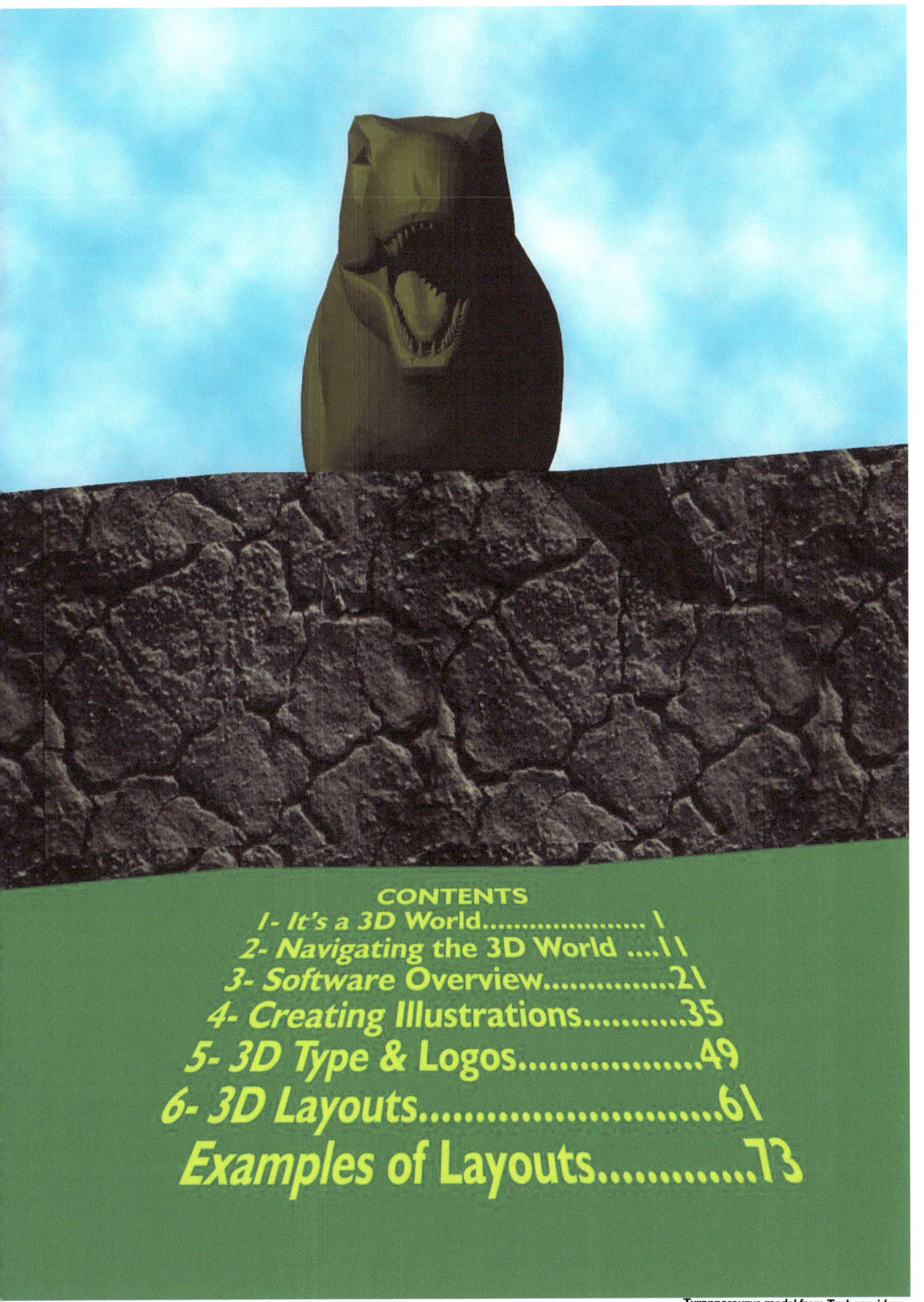

## CONTENTS

# CHAPTER I

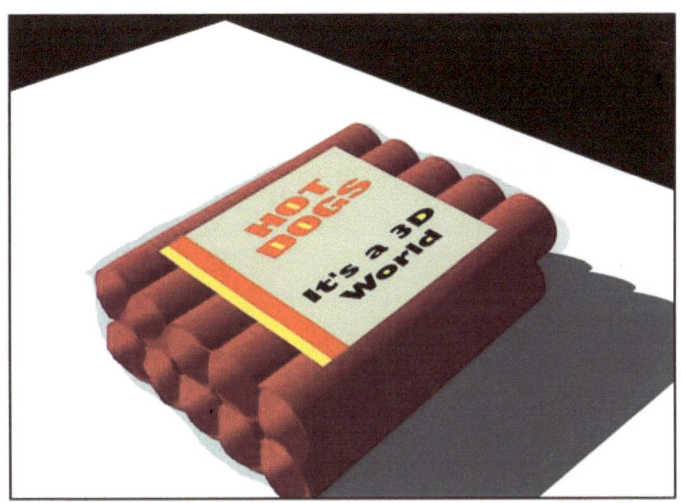

*A* tidal wave of information and entertainment crashes onto the shores of our lives every day . . . big-budget films about heroes and the end of the world . . . gripping television coverage of live news events, squeezed between popular shows and seductive commercials . . . bulky newspapers offering a rich serving of news, features and advertising . . . supermarket tabloids promising to reveal the dirty secrets of celebrities and politicians . . . intriguing web pages on the Internet . . . personalized content transmitted directly to cell phones and other hand-held devices . . .

The assault on our senses will intensify as the Internet expands, new cable television channels move into American homes, and advertising agencies devise more ingenious ways to seduce consumers. In this visually oriented, fragmented society, how can *your* front page, magazine cover, advertisement, brochure or poster grab people by

# 3D IN PRINT

their collars and shake them out of their lethargy? How can print publications, faced with rising costs and dwindling audiences, convince consumers to actually *read* their scintillating prose? Must they embrace the lowest common denominators of public taste and entertainment to compete effectively?

No! There is a better way . . .

This is where 3D comes in.

Nothing is more important to the success of your enterprise than the quality of the content or product, but three-dimensional graphics are one of the tools that can give your printed pages a unique look and a competitive edge.

In the last twenty years, 3D software has become much more powerful and affordable. Software that runs on home computers (provided you have enough processor speed, memory and hard drive space) is also used to create special effects for major motion pictures and television shows. The blockbuster film *Titanic* was created with the help of Softimage I 3D, LightWave 3D and Alias I Wavefront's Power Animator. Softimage and Alias I Wavefront's Dynamation served up special effects in *Twister*. Alias I Wavefront and Softimage added an extra dimension to *Dragonheart*. Maya, Softimage and Power Animator helped bring Disney's *Dinosaur* to life.

To produce interesting 3D effects for a print publication, you do not need to shell out thousands of dollars for expensive software that comes with all the bells and whistles, like animation. Other applications offer terrific graphic capabilities at less cost.

Some publications already use 3D extensively. Check out the graphics in *USA Today*, or in 3D print magazines such as *CGW* (*Computer Graphics World*) and *3D World*, or 3D online magazines such as *3dcreative* and *CGIndia* (see chapter 3).

# 3D IN PRINT

A dazzling array of 3D tools are available, but 2D print media have only scratched the surface when it comes to using these tools creatively and effectively . . .

■ Too often, editors or designers simply plop a three-dimensional graphic on a page, flow type around it and hurriedly ship the page off to the printer.

■ Three-dimensional logos or headlines are capriciously slapped onto two-dimensional layouts. The 3D element often sticks out like a sumo wrestler at a Girl Scout convention.

■ More commonly, print designers on deadline avoid 3D tools entirely, believing they are complicated and time-consuming.

Time to wake up and see what 3D can do for your publication! Consider this . . .

■ Three-dimensional graphics add impact to publications and help them communicate effectively. Instead of using a 2D drawing of a proposed football stadium, render it in 3D for a more realistic view of what the stadium will look like. Instead of using a 2D photo of a product in an advertisement, create the product in a 3D program for maximum clarity and control over lighting and shadows. When you need another shot of the product, perhaps for use in a brochure, use the same model viewed from a different angle or in a different setting.

■ Facing a deadline and there's not enough time to create a sophisticated 3D graphic? Even someone with limited illustration experience may find that some 3D

# 3D IN PRINT

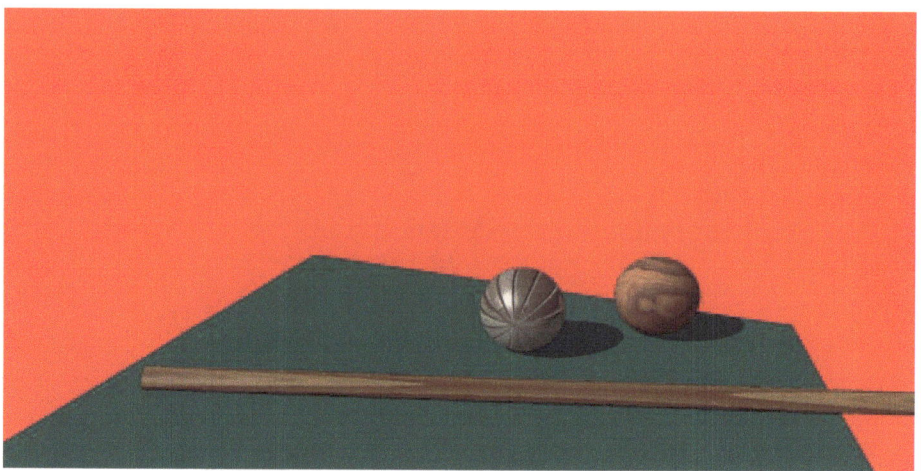

*Texture mapping and photorealistic rendering make it possible to create a simple 3D scene quickly.*

programs are easier to use than 2D drawing programs. Creating a simple photorealistic illustration to accompany a story can be as easy as drawing a shape, adding a texture and rendering. For instance, the billiard table illustration above was created quickly in Strata 3d software on the Macintosh.

■ Or, the image you need might be available on the Internet as 3D clip art. Thousands of sophisticated images can be downloaded quickly for free or for a fee. (Be sure to determine whether you need permission to use the models in commercial print media.)

■ Another option: If you need a realistic 3D rendering of a specific object that isn't available as clip art—perhaps a building or a car—applications such as ImageModeler and PhotoModeler allow you to use photos of the object to create a 3D model without actually drawing it. (See "3D Models from Photos" in chapter 3.)

■ If you are looking for wonderfully crafted human figures, complete with clothes

# 3D IN PRINT

and hair, check out Poser, from SmithMicro Software.

■ And, there are times when you should think about the whole package—graphics, photographs, headlines, body type and sidebars—in terms of three dimensions.

What you do with 3D software is up to you. In *The Kingdom and the Power*, Gay Talese notes that Iphigene Ochs Sulzberger, daughter of *New York Times* publisher Adolph Ochs, told a story about a medieval traveler who came upon three stonecutters. The traveler asked each what he was doing. The first stonecutter said he was cutting stone. The second said he was making a corner stone. The third said he was building a cathedral. In a way, that's how it is when three people all use the same software. To one, it is a means to create extruded type or a simple model. To another, it might be a vehicle for creating an intriguing 3D scene. But a third illustrator—the cathedral builder—might use the same software over a period of days or weeks to create complex scenes or even massive projects, such as the design of Hong Kong's multi-billion dollar airport or a detailed virtual model of Philadelphia. (Large projects are discussed in more detail in chapter 4.) You may not have the time or motivation to develop such elaborate projects, but your 3D software may be quite capable of creating them!

When dealing with 3D elements in print publications, resist the urge to use 3D for everything. Sometimes it is inappropriate, or juvenilistic. Many illustrations and layouts do not lend themselves to effective 3D presentation. 3D should not be a gimmick, but an integral part of the layout. Like other elements of design, it should arise out of content nat-

# 3D IN PRINT

urally, just as Frank Lloyd Wright's prairie houses seem to rise naturally from their surroundings.

This is an idea book, intended to stimulate creativity. Hopefully, it will inspire those who are interested in designing print media, whether they are professional designers, overworked editors, freelancers, or students.

Making an ad, poster, or print publication more dynamic and exciting does not need to involve spending a lot of money. The cost of 3D software is reasonable. The creativity that produces those dynamic and exciting ideas can come from people already on the payroll.

Here is what you will find in the pages ahead . . .

In chapter 2, differences in 3D interfaces are examined. How do you find an interface you are comfortable with? What should you look for? We also will consider different types of modeling, and a few of the advanced features offered by 3D applications.

In chapter 3, software is compared. After looking at complete modeling, rendering and animation packages, we will consider applications that specialize in modeling terrain, transforming 2D photos into 3D and painting on 3D models. Sources of 3D clip art and textures also are listed.

Chapter 4 discusses working in the 3D world. The wonderful thing about 3D packages is that they handle a lot of the work for you. You must come up with the fundamental idea—the basic design—but the program will take care of perspective and rendering. We also will look at many types of 3D artwork, from simple models, to the human face and figure, to major projects.

Chapter 5 explores 3D type and logos, one of

# 3D IN PRINT

the most common uses of 3D in contemporary publications. If handled well, the effects can be stunning. A few possibilities: giving your type shadows, filling it, mapping it with textures, massaging it, giving it perspective, or plastering it on 3D objects.

And, finally, chapter 6 focuses on 3D layouts. We will see how graphics, type and headlines come together to make a cohesive layout. Rough layouts illustrating many aspects of 3D illustration and page design are included.

Let's begin with a look at some of the 3D interfaces on the market . . .

# CHAPTER 2

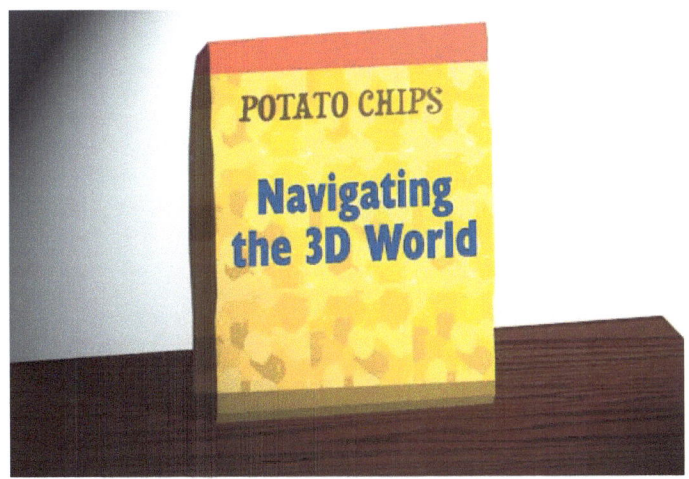

—

**T**rying out a 3D application is like test-driving a new car. The prospective buyer should kick the tires, look under the hood and take it out on the road to see how it performs at full speed. Tryout versions of many 3D titles are available for free downloading on the Internet.

During our search for a 3D application we will consider various approaches to modeling and differences in user interfaces. We also will look at advanced features, as well as factors to consider if you plan to use your models on the Internet.

Start by making sure you possess the necessary computer hardware and operating system software. Some applications run only on the PC, others only on the Macintosh.

Determine whether your computer can muster all the processor speed, RAM and hard drive space the application requires. And be sure the 3D software is compatible with the version of the operating system software installed on your computer.

## Approaches to Modeling

Some 3D software makes it easy to create simple shapes, add depth, plaster them with sophisticated textures and render them with a slick photo-realistic look. Graphics like this are immensely useful for editors and designers in a hurry. More advanced features are buried deeper in the program.

On the other hand, software packages with difficult or awkward interfaces can be frustrating unless the user has the time and patience to master the software.

Creating a cone, for example, is relatively easy in some applications. Click on the cone primitive in the toolbox, click in the working window and a cone appears. Drag a texture onto the cone and render it. But creating the same cone in other applications can be more complicated. In the first version of Impulse, Inc.'s Imagine, for example, the user would access an editing screen, select Functions/Add/Primitive from a menu, and a Primitive Types requester appeared. After clicking on the Cone button, a Cone Parameters requester appeared. The user could accept the default size of the cone or change the parameters. Then, the user returned to the Detail Editor and a wireframe cone appeared on the screen. To move the cone, the user couldn't just drag it in the window. He had to click on a control point in the center of the cone, click on the MOV button at the bottom of the screen, and then drag the cone to its new position. Color was added to the cone by accessing the Attributes Requester and clicking on the color button so the red, green and blue sliders and data input boxes became active. The user adjusted the slider or entered data in the boxes to select a color, then clicked on the OK button and returned to the Detail Editor. To render the cone, the user selected Project/Quickrender and a Quickrender Lighting requester appeared. The user clicked the OK button to accept the default lighting and the cone was rendered.

In addition to considering the complexity involved in creating 3D models, you will want to evaluate the different approaches applications take to modeling. These might include primitives, polygonal modeling, spline modeling, "sculpting" with organic modelers, subdivision surface modeling and a long list of modeling tools, often including lathing, extrusion, sweeping, deformation and Boolean operations (which use intersecting parts of objects to carve out new shapes).

### ■ Polygonal Modeling

Some lower-level applications rely on primitives such as spheres, boxes, cylinders and cones, creating complex shapes by combining, deforming, or performing Boolean operations on them. The models are then saved as polygons.

More sophisticated modelers use a combination of primitives and 2D and 3D drawing tools to create models. Complex graphics may consist of hundreds of thousands of polygons, resulting in very large files and lengthy rendering times.

### ■ Spline-Based Modeling

Because polygons do not accurately represent true curves, many designers prefer applications that support splines—lines with multiple control points. Splines fall into three general categories:

*Linear splines,* in which control points are connected by straight lines.

*Interpolating splines,* which always touch the points that control them.

*Approximating splines,* which can have a soft curve and which do not necessarily touch the control points. B-splines and NURBS (Non-Uniform Rational B-splines) are approximating splines. Rhino is an

# 3D IN PRINT

example of a Windows-based application that supports NURBS modeling.

MetaNURBS is an attempt to combine the best features of polygonal and spline modeling. A polygonal-type mesh is formed around the spline model.

Cinema 4D offers extensive polygon modeling tools which can be used to create complex objects. Among them: a knife tool, stitch and sew tool and brush and magnet tools. HyperNURBS smooths polygonal models for a more organic appearance.

In LightWave's Modeler, you can work with points or polygons. Many modification tools are included for working with them. LightWave offers not only the usual primitive objects but others such as gears and seashells.

Carrara offers a spline modeler, a polygonal modeler and a metaball modeler. Modeling tools include the Boolean tool, edge and surfaces tools, and curve tools.

Amorphium's subdivision surface modeling uses a control cage to shape models. Any part of the model can be subdivided into smaller areas of control.

Modeling in Nendo uses a "digital clay" sculpting type of environment to create objects.

## The User Interface

In addition to evaluating the application's approach to modeling, you will want to consider the user interface. It is through the user interface that you interact with an application. How easy is it to create fairly simple models quickly? How difficult is it to access and use the software's more powerful features? How are the tools arranged in the main window? Are other features of the program grouped

# 3D IN PRINT

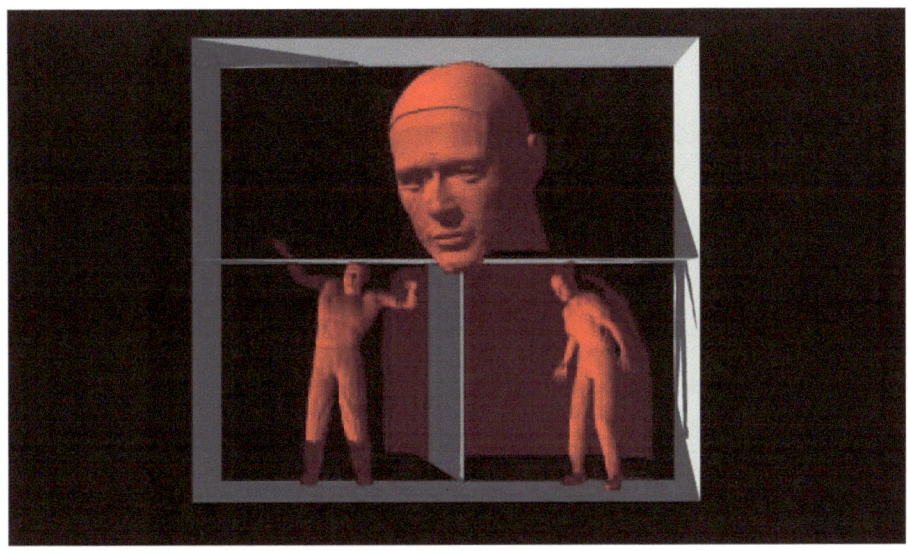

logically and are they easily accessible? How difficult is it to navigate through the software?

Many of today's 3D applications trace their
roots back to the 1980s. when a meg of RAM was a
big deal. Colin Olson's 3D-Edit, a shareware modeler
for the Macintosh, recommended that 512K be available for the program. Like many 3D applications
that would follow, 3D-Edit employed four simul-
taneous on-screen views—top, front, right and the
final drawing screen—and featured tools for building models from primitives and tools for drawing
irregular objects.

As computers became more powerful,
equipped with additional RAM, bigger hard drives
and faster processors, 3D software grew more sophisticated. Even so, applications usually retained the
basic interface they started with. New features were
layered on the original program because develop-
ers wanted upgrades to be compatible with earlier
versions. It is important to find an interface you
are comfortable with, because if you stay with one

application, you may be working in the same interface for years.

Although capabilities of 3D programs vary
widely, many of the interfaces bear similarities.
Menus usually can be accessed along the top of the
screen and tool icons along the left side. A large
working area in the middle often can be subdivided
into multiple views. Key elements of the program
often can be lined up down the right side. In Strata
3D CX, the right side can be used for lists of exten-
sions, object properties, environment settings, and
so on. In Carrara, the side elements are called trays.
3D programs often allow users to rearrange interface
elements.

## ■ One Workspace or Separate Modules?

Generally, the trend in 3D interfaces has moved
from the modular approach to interfaces in which
more takes place in the primary working area. Light-
Wave 3D, which uses separate Modeler and Layout
programs, has connected the two much more closely,
so changes in the Modeler are immediately available
in Layout. Models are created and surface materials
applied in the Modeler; in the Layout Editor, camera
and lights are added, objects positioned in the scene,
and animation and rendering are set up. The Hub—
where scene file data is stored—is accessible from
both the Modeler and Layout.

Poser and Carrara prefer to use "rooms" where
you can work on specialized aspects of your project.
In Carrara, rooms are for assembling, modeling, sto-
ryboarding, texturing and rendering. In Poser, you
can work on characters in the Poser Room, Material
Room, Face Room, Hair Room, Cloth Room, Setup
Room, etc.

# 3D IN PRINT

## ■ Advanced Features

In addition to basic modeling, rendering and animation capabilities, many 3D applications offer a varied fare of advanced features. These include support for scripting, which improves productivity by automating tasks; 64-bit processing; UV editing; faster and better rendering technologies; and integration with such programs as Adobe Illustrator, Adobe Photoshop, Adobe After Effects and Final Cut Pro.

Other advanced features include realistic special effects such as fur; fog, smoke, glow and mist; wind and gravity controls; sophisticated types of mapping and texture handling; depth of field; and constraints, which are a way of relating one object to another without the limits imposed by hierarchy. Many applications support plug-ins from third-party suppliers.

## ■ Saving Your Work

Some applications can save your models in numerous formats for exporting to other 3D programs. Among the formats: DXF (the Drawing eXchange Format), .3ds (3D Studio), 3DMF (Quick-Draw 3D format), IGES (Initial Graphics Exchange Specifications standard), VRML, OBJ, .lwo (Light-Wave) and Amapi.

After you render your creation, you might want to save the rendering in a form recognized by image editing, page layout and word processing programs. Many 3D programs save output in TIFF, PICT, EPS, JPEG, BMP and PCX formats.

## ■ Go Deep Into the Program

Try your hand at navigating the 3D world using various software. Download demo versions of many applications from the Web. Find an interface that is comfortable for you. If one application does not meet your requirements, perhaps two will. After you decide which software to purchase, embrace it as your own. *Go deep.* Any 3D program will serve you better if you learn as much about its capabilities as you can.

## The Web Connection

Most newspapers and magazines have web sites. The 3D content which they create for their print publications can also be used on the Internet. In addition, specialized 3D applications are designed to create content specifically for the web.

Over the years, the obstacle to widespread use of 3D on the web has been the problem of how to deliver the 3D content in a form that the user's browser can handle. Today, numerous avenues for delivery of 3D over the Internet are available, but the ideal—that all web browsers should be able to handle 3D graphics without special plug-ins or applets—has not be achieved. Webmasters must take into consideration how many users' browsers will be able to handle their 3D content if plug-ins or applets are required. Software such as Adobe Director can be used to create and publish interactive content for the web.

If you wish to simply post a picture of a 3D graphic on your web site, it is very easy, of course. Just save the graphic in jpeg or png format and insert it into the web page as you would any other graphic.

# CHAPTER 3

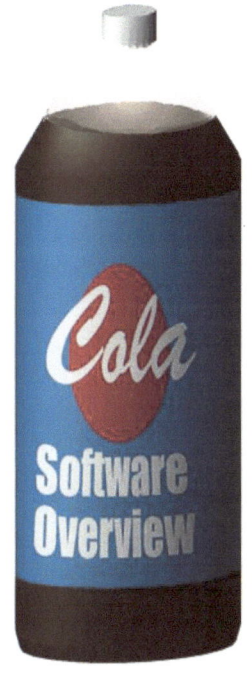

*B*efore choosing your 3D weapon, you might want to inspect the arsenal.

In this chapter is an overview of 3D software packages, followed by a look at specialized applications and a list of popular print and online 3D magazines. Tryout versions of most 3D applications are available on their web sites.

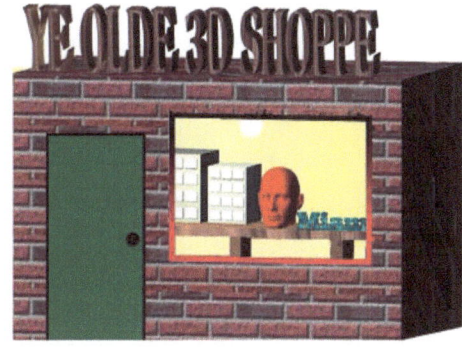

A note of caution: consult the Internet for the latest software developments because the 3D software picture changes frequently. Also, be aware that Microsoft and Apple update their operating system software frequently. If you decide to upgrade your 3D software, you might need to purchase new operating system software to run it.

## ■ Pricing

Because prices and version numbers change frequently, they are not generally listed below, but here are some tips on what to expect:

Whatever the size of your budget, you should be able to find a 3D program in your price range.

# 3D IN PRINT

Mail order and academic prices usually are lower. And many companies offer special deals on their web sites.

You might save money by buying an entry-level version of a product and then upgrading to the more powerful application. And a few 3D applications are free.

The following list notes whether the software is available for computers running Macintosh and/or Windows operating systems. Check the company's web site to determine which versions of the Windows or Macintosh operating systems the software supports. Some software packages support additional operating systems.

## 3D Applications

**AC3D** [MAC, WIN] features a simple user interface, Truetype font 2D and 3D generator, and fast subdivision surface modeling. It supports many 3D file formats. Inivis Limited  www.inivis.org

**Amorphium** [MAC, WIN] is low-price software with an intuitive interface. It features real time 3D sculpting and painting. It's like using digital clay. Company literature states, "it's the only tool that can give your models that essential dose of reality in no time flat. From dents to dings, from scratches to scrapes, from crinkles to collisions, Amorphium lets you actually apply geometry detail to solid shaded objects with a real-time airbrush." In other words, it can take a perfect model of a car and wreck it for you in less than an hour.  EI Technology Group www.amorphium.com

**Autodesk 3ds Max** [WIN] is a leader in 3D graphics. It offers multiple modeling tools, comprehensive materials editing and workstation-quality rendering and animation. It has been used to create

# 3D IN PRINT

games, video and film content. If you are on a limited budget and interested primarily in preparing simple 3D illustrations for print, purchasing 3ds Max would be like buying a Rolls Royce for a trip to the grocery. Autodesk www.autodesk.com

**Autodesk Maya** [MAC, WIN] is an expensive and versatile modeling, rendering and animation package. It includes NURBS and polygon modeling, Artisan tools for sculpting and modeling using a brush, and Interactive Photorealistic Rendering (IPR). Maya 2010 includes all the features of Maya Complete and Maya Unlimited as well as new advanced features. A personal learning edition of Maya is available. Autodesk www.autodesk.com

**Autodesk Softimage** [WIN] is a high-end application that offers ICE (Interactive Creative Environment), which Autodesk says is a groundbreaking technology that transforms XSI into a powerful and flexible open platform. Among Softimage features: NURBS modeling, innovative organic modeling techniques, high quality rendering, polygon and color reduction, 3D painting, and character animation and special effects. Autodesk www.autodesk.com

**Blender** [MAC, WIN] is a free 3D graphics application with an unusual interface that has been around since 1994. It can be used for modeling, UV unwrapping, texturing, rigging, animating, etc. Also available for other operating systems. The Blender Foundation www.blender.org

**Bonzai3D** [MAC, WIN] is a relatively simple modeler designed to create fast but robust models. It is aimed at delivering conceptual designs on the fly while maintaining the option to transform them into accurate and robust models. AutoDesSys, Inc. www.bonzai3d.com

**Carrara** [MAC, WIN] A single solution for realistic figure posing and animation combined with

# 3D IN PRINT

advanced modeling, terrain-building, physics and multi-pass rendering. Daz 3d www.daz3d.com

**Cheetah 3D** [MAC] boasts powerful modeling, rendering and animation capabilities. Intuitive interface, UV editing. Written for Mac OS X. www.cheetah3d.com

**Cinema 4D** [MAC, WIN] offers an easy-to-use, intuitive interface. The core application contains everything you need to create high-end 3D images and animations. For artists whose work demands more, seamlessly integrated modules are available. MAXON Computer www.maxon.net

**DAZ Studio** [MAC, WIN] is a free application with a Quick Start interface. It includes lip-Sync, a start-up wizard, multiple UVs and three complete scenes of 3D content. Daz 3d www.daz3d.com

**form•z** [MAC, WIN] is a versatile application with a steep learning curve that can handle both surface and solids modeling. It includes photorealistic rendering and Metaformz, which applies metaball behavior to a variety of shapes. AutoDesSys, Inc. www.formz.com

**LightWave 3D** [MAC, WIN] emphasizes speed, flexibility and value. Offers powerful modeling, animation, rendering and special effects capabilities. Used in Hollywood film production and broadcast TV production. It is probably overkill for the ordinary print designer. Newtek, Inc. www.newtek.com/LightWave

**Mirai** [WIN] features a suite of real-time content creation tools. Includes subdivision surface modeling and smoothing algorithms. You can work like a sculptor, modeling and texturing a "rough" version of an object before transforming it into a smooth model instantly. Izware www.izware.com

**MODO** [MAC, WIN] provides 3D modeling, painting and rendering in a single integrated and accelerated package. It features a fast polygonal and subdivision surface 3D modeler. Integrated sculpting tools are provided alongside traditional modeling tools. Luxology LLC  www.luxology.com

**Nendo** [WIN] is an easy to use 3D modeling and painting package. Model in a "digital clay" environment, working within an interface based on traditional sculpting. Create organic as well as hard-edged objects. Izware  www.izware.com

**Pixels 3D** [MAC] is a versatile modeling and rendering software. It includes special effects such as fur, ShaderMaker Pro and a raytrace renderer. Pixels Digital  www.pixels3d.com

**Strata 3D CX** [MAC, WIN] is a powerful, easy-to-use modeling, rendering and animation package. Incontext modeling makes modeling easy to control in the main window. Features include a wide selection of modeling tools, texture compositing, fast scanline rendering, particle effects, many rendering options and volumetric shaders for aura, fog, mist and haze. Extensive import and export file support. The latest version allows users to incorporate 3D with Adobe Photoshop CS3 and CS4. Strata www.strata3d.com

**trueSpace** [WIN] offers modeling, rendering and animating in one workspace. Features include real-time preview, drawing in 3D, painting on surfaces and shaping objects like clay. Includes Booleans, UV editor, morphs, etc. Caligari Corporation www.caligari.com

## Terrain Builders

**Bryce 3D** [MAC, WIN] creates realistic environments that can be populated with human figures and animals. Using a unique, functional interface, the user can create landscape backgrounds that include trees, rippling water, realistic mountains, snow and rocky textures. Daz 3d   www.daz3d.com

**MojoWorld** [MAC, WIN] can create photorealistic landscapes. MojoWorld Focus allows you to insert yourself and others into incredible new worlds. Pandromeda, Inc. www.pandromeda.com

**Vue** [MAC, WIN] creates, renders and animates realistic 3D scenery. The basic version, Pioneer, was free when we checked on it. e-on software  www.e-onsoftware.com

**World Builder** [WIN] features tools for precise landscape creation and editing. Handles water, mountains, grass, stones, etc.   Digital Element www.digi-element.com

**World Construction Set** [WIN] imports terrain in various file formats, or you can build a scene from scratch using a fractal terrain generator. The program offers real world, GIS (Geographic Information Systems) based tools and real world ecosystems. Graphics of plants and trees included. **Visual Nature Studio** [WIN] is a more powerful, more complex and more expensive package for power users. 3dnature www.3dnature.com

## 3d Models From Photos

**Autodesk ImageModeler** [WIN] generates photorealistic 3D models from 2D digital images with real-world accuracy. Utilizes a three-step workflow—calibration, modeling and texturing.   Autodesk www.autodesk.com

**Canoma** [MAC, WIN] allows fast creation of photorealistic 3D models from one or more photographs. The models are geometrically simple, and allow fast 3D prototyping. Adobe acquired Canoma and it is not being sold at this time, but copies occasionally are available on the Internet.`

# 3D IN PRINT

**Strata Foto 3D** [MAC, WIN] creates 3D content from still images. Photos of an object on a printed mat are taken from a number of viewpoints. The shape of the object and its surface color are automatically extracted from each photo and the information is used to build a high quality 3D object. The model can be sent to a 3D layer in Photoshop CS3 or CS4 EX or imported into 3D editing and rendering software such as Strata 3D CX. Strata  www.strata3d.com

**PhotoModeler** [WIN] builds accurate 3D models of real-world objects and scenes using two or more overlapping photos from different angles. Photo-Modeler is the base product. PhotoModeler Automation adds coded targets and project automation. PhotoModeler Scanner contains the capabilities of PhotoModeler and PhotoModeler Automation, and adds scanning and dense surface modeling.  Eos Systems  www.photomodeler.com

## Character Creation

**Evolver**   [WIN] The user interface of Evolver is available at no charge.  You are able to design an unlimited number of characters and save those designs.  When you want to generate a design, that is when you are charged. If you are taking characters from Evolver into a 3D graphics package and want the full source to the character, the charge at present is $189.  You get four resolutions of mesh, texture files, full skeletal rig, and full facial rig. Darwin also was planning to allow Evolver to be run in a browser, making it compatible with all platforms. Darwin Dimensions www.darwindimensions.com

**FaceShop** [MAC, WIN] functions as a plug-in that works inside DAZ Studio or as a standalone application. Tools include a MorphBrush and TextureBrush. FaceShop Pro is a stand-alone application that allows

# 3D IN PRINT

you to create a unique 3D head from any photo, re-creating the original camera angle for accuracy. Also available: a FaceShop Photoshop Plug-in, FaceShop 3D Camera Systems and FaceMaker.  Abalone LLC www.abalonellc.com

**Quidam** [MAC, WIN] is for fast creation and modeling of 3D characters. You start with a new base character or starting point, not from scratch. Each character's body parts can be changed. You can add hair, clothes, shoes and jewelry to enhance them. N-Sided  www.n-sided.com

**Poser** [MAC, WIN] creates high-resolution models of the human form with high-quality surface mapping (cover your models with clothes). Now includes animal models, hair and character animation with facial expression. Poser Pro is geared toward production environments  Smith Micro Software  www.smithmicro.com.

## Photoshop Plug-ins

Many 3D-oriented plug-ins are available for Photoshop, such as the **Andromeda Series 2 filters**. Others include:

**Aurora**, for creating 3D skies with clouds, water reflections, etc.

**3D Bridge**, for working interactively with 3D objects in DAZ Studio and seeing real-time results in Photoshop.

**Strata Plug-ins for Photoshop**
**LightWave Rendition**, a render plug-in.

## 3D Clip Art

(For additional sources of clip art, see www.3dlinks.com)

**www.baument.com**
**www.cacheforce.com**

# 3D IN PRINT

www.digimation.com
www.linefour.com
www.marlinstudios.com
www.ModelMasters.com
www.poitra.com
www.Templates.com
www.TurboSquid.com
www.zygote.com

## Terrain Maps

**Map Resources** distributes editable vector maps in Adobe Illustrator and PDF format. Map Resources  www.mapresources.com

**Mountain High Maps** offers relief maps (detailed and accurate map views of the world's continents, countries and ocean floors.) Digital Wisdom, Inc.  www.mountainhighmaps.com

## 3D Fonts

**Effect3D Studio** [WIN] gives you the power to create stunning 3D text objects simply by typing in your text.   reallusion, inc. www.reallusion.com

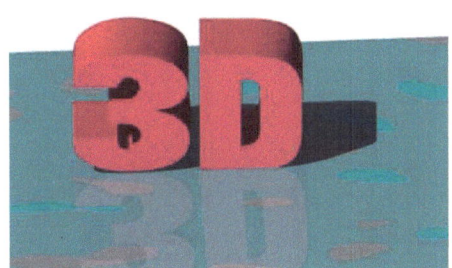

**TypeStyler** [MAC] offers type effects that include embossing, transparency, glow, metal type, bump mapping, soft shadows, picture fills and much more. Strider Software  www.typestyler.com

## 3D Textures

(also see www.3dlinks.com for sources of textures.)

www.artbeats.com
www.marlinstudios.com

# 3D IN PRINT

## Painting on 3D Models

**BodyPaint 3D** offers control over your textures with complete layers, filters and tablet support. You can paint on up to ten channels with a single stroke, so a brush can define an entire material rather than a single color. Plus, RayBrush technology lets you view the results of your painting real time in a rendered image. MAXON Computer www.maxon.net

**ZBrush** [MAC, WIN] is a digital sculpting and painting program. Allows you to paint in two or three dimensions. It features a depth-sensitive drawing surface and visual feedback in real time. Pixologic, Inc. www.pixologic.com

## Rendering

**PolyTrans** and **NuGraf** [WIN] are rendering and data translation applications. NuGraf contains the functionality of Poly Trans plus material and texture editing, multi-threaded ray tracing, font creation, etc. Okino Computer Graphics www.okino.com

**Persistence of Vision Ray Tracer (POV-Ray)** [MAC, WIN] can be downloaded free from the web site. Persistence of Vision Ray Tracer Pty., Ltd. www.povray.org

## 3D Magazines

For the latest 3D news and reviews, check out magazines such as these:

**3dcreative** A downloadable PDF magazine. Quality tutorials, interviews, techniques, galleries, etc. Subscriptions available at the web site. 144-page issue in February, 2009. www.3dcreativemag.com

**3D World** Slick print magazine from Britain. www.3dworldmag.com

# 3D IN PRINT

**CGIndia**  High quality online graphics magazine. www.cgindia.org

**CGW** (**Computer Graphics World***)  A print publication. Also, a web site at www.cgw.com

**HDRI 3D**  A print magazine published 6 times a year.  DMG Publishing  www.hdri3d.com

**High End Magazine**  Specialized magazines dealing with animation, rendering, special effects and specific software such as Cinema 4D also are available. www.highendmag.com

For a comprehensive list of commercial and free 3D magazines and newsletters, see 3dlinks.com.

# CHAPTER 4

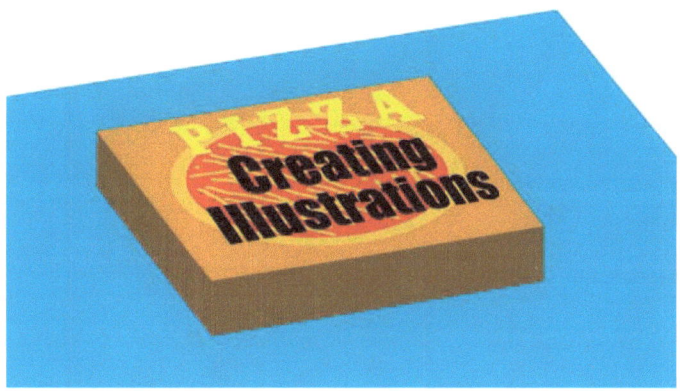

In the 3D environment, most applications label the horizontal axis x, the vertical y, and the depth axis z. The origin point of the 3D universe is 0,0,0. In many applications, you can specify coordinates of an object in a dialog box. Every object, camera and light has a position and orientation relative to the origin point.

Traditionally, 3D programs have offered the viewer the choice of working with multiple views of the object simultaneously or working in a single view. Working in a single isometric view offers three-point perspective; the depth in the 3D scene becomes apparent. It will quickly become obvious, however, that other viewpoints are necessary. Objects may seem to touch when viewed from a single viewpoint, but another view may reveal they are separated by a large distance.

A word about perspective: *One-point perspective* is the view you have of an object or scene if

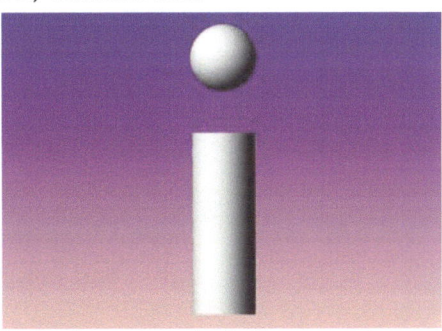

*In the front view, the ball seems to be over the cylinder. In a side view, the ball is seen to be behind the cylinder.*

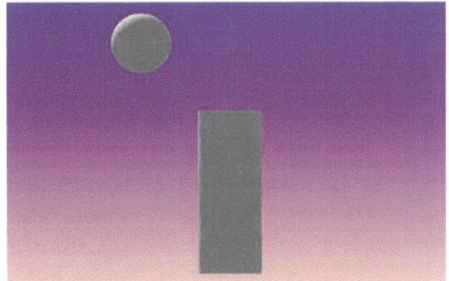

# 3D IN PRINT

you are looking at it straight on, not from an angle. If extended, perspective lines converge at a single Vanishing Point in the distance. *Two-point perspective* is the view you have if you observe the object or scene from an angle. Perspective lines trail off to two points in the distance. In *three-point perspective*, the observer sees the object or scene from an angle, as in two-point perspective, but the observer is looking on the scene from down low or up high. Perspective lines converge at three different Vanishing Points.

3D programs make the task of capturing the exact view you seek of a scene easier by allowing the positioning of cameras and lights, either manually or through dialog boxes. Targeting the camera or light to the scene is helpful when you plan to reposition the camera, light or elements in the scene.

Some programs let you adjust the controls on the virtual camera, allowing you to control how much of the scene you capture in the final rendering.

Don't neglect lighting. The type of lighting and the placement of lights can affect the appearance of a scene dramatically. Spotlights can add harsh light and dark shadows to a scene. Lamps can give the same scene soft, selective illumination. Among the types of lighting are ambient lights, spotlights, point lights and lamps.

## Your 3D Models

.    Objects for your scenes can be created in your 3D application or imported from other sources.

■ Simple 3D models can be created easily using primitives—a block, cylinder, sphere or cone, for example.

■ More complex models can be constructed and manipulated using the application's modeling tools. As noted in chapter 2, 3D applications embrace a

# 3D IN PRINT

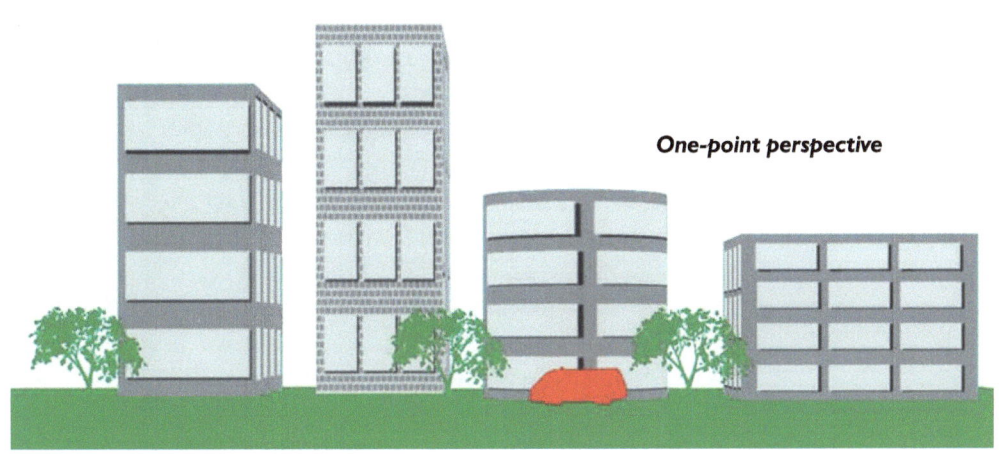

*One-point perspective*

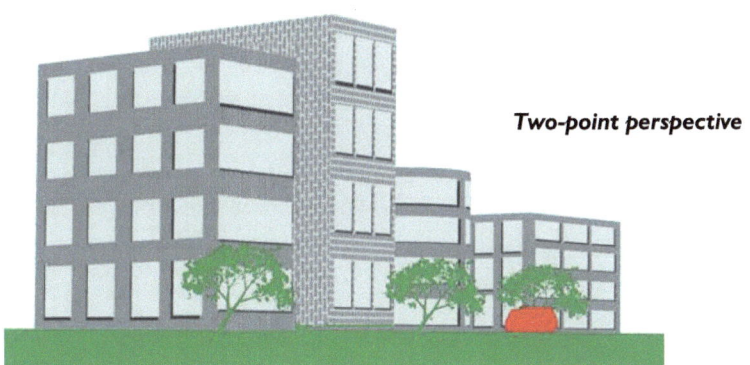

*Two-point perspective*

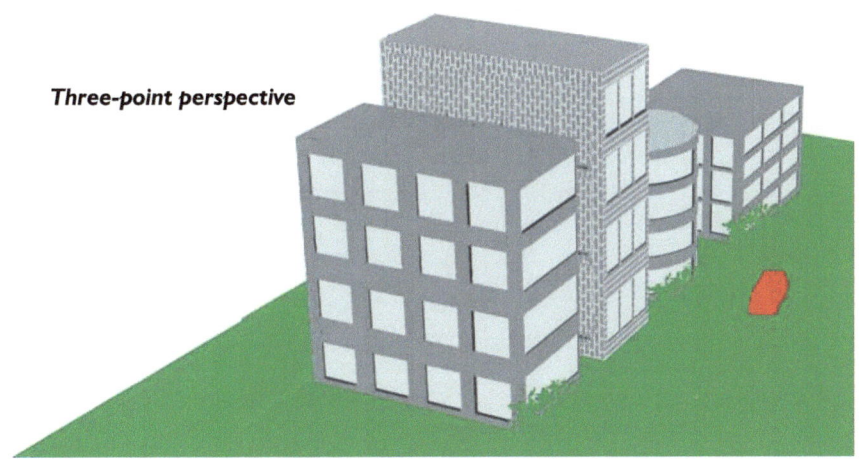

*Three-point perspective*

wide range of modeling methods. Shapes also can be joined to make a whole. Skinning (also called lofting) can be used to join objects by stretching a skin over them.

■ You can import 3D models to use in your scenes. These include models you create in other 3D applications; 3D clip art from the Internet or other sources; models of real objects created by 3D digitizers and scanners; and models imported from applications specializing in creating 3D objects from photographs. Applications usually import 3D models in a variety of formats, such as DXF, 3DMF (QuickDraw 3D format), VRML, 3ds, OBJ, Amapi and .lwo (LightWave) And, they can import files in 2D formats—such as TIFF, PICT, JPEG, EPS and BMP—to use as textures or objects without depth, or for conversion into 3D objects.

## ■ Planning Saves Time

Analyze a 3D project before starting it. What is the best way to create the model? From primitives? From splines? NURBS or MetaNURBS? Using skinning, lathing, or Boolean operations? How many parts do you want to break the model down into for modeling? Do you have the textures you will need, or must you create, import or scan more textures? Is the best way to create the model also fast enough to ensure you will finish before your deadline?

If you know where you are going, you will get there faster.

## ■ Textures

One of the keys to producing realistic objects is texture mapping. Many applications offer sophis-

# 3D IN PRINT

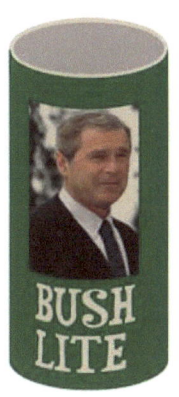

ticated mapping procedures that allow you to define the type of mapping, the tiling (if any) and the quality and texture of the map.

The inventory of textures at your disposal in your 3D application expands considerably when you import scanned images or 2D images created in other applications.

Sometimes you know there's something wrong with your model but you can't put your finger on the problem. It is drawn well, the textures are bright and colorful, it looks almost perfect . . . and that may be the problem. Through textures, you can make your model look old, used or imperfect.

## ■ Painting on 3D Models

Some 3D applications ship with 3D painting capabilities. You also can use specialized applications for painting on 3D models. Among them: Deep Paint 3D and ZBrush. (See chapter 3).

## ■ Building the Scene

A scene is created by combining models on one central stage. Elements are positioned relative to one another. Some are linked in parent-child relationships.

Backgrounds can be set up in the program or imported.

## ■ Rendering

This is the icing on the cake. Depending on your software, the 3D scene can be rendered in many ways—and the quality of the finished artwork can vary dramatically. Some applications support features such as fur, fog, mist, haze and depth of field, as well as multiple textures on an object. Anti-aliasing smoothes out annoying jaggles.

If your project does not require photorealistic

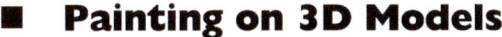

# 3D IN PRINT

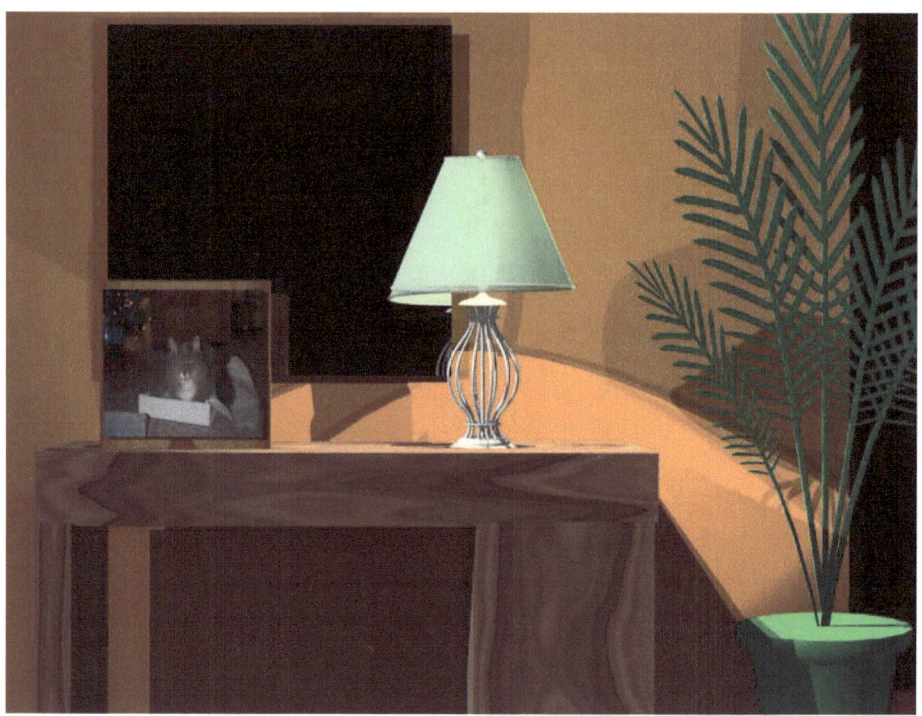

*A textured scene rendered with light from a lamp. Notice the photo of a cat. (His name is Boomer.)*

rendering, some applications offer cel rendering, for a cartoonish effect.

Check out the finished artwork from various programs to find the rendering quality that suits your needs. If your budget allows, you might prefer to use software that specializes in rendering.

## ■ Final Effects

Adobe Photoshop and similar graphic retouching programs are invaluable tools for 3D. You can easily touch up your final renderings. Effects that would be time-consuming or impossible in 3D applications are sometimes handled easily by these programs.

# 3D IN PRINT

## Examples of 3D Art

Publications can benefit from many types of 3D illustrations, depending on their needs at the moment. A simple illustration on deadline? No problem. A more complex photorealistic artwork? A cinch. How about "coming at you" graphics that seem to leap off the page? Or a human figure with the face of a celebrity? No problem.

**Simple Illustrations**—Your deadline is a half hour away and the artwork you were counting on didn't arrive. Where can you find an illustration ASAP? You might create a quick and dirty graphic in a 3D application. How about drawing a label in a 2D graphics program and wrapping it around a can? Or, for a chess article, texture-mapping a box with photos of chess players?

If you require a simple graphic depicting a proposed structure, 3D programs often produce suitable models faster than 2D programs. When Chicago's Mayor Daley proposed putting a retractable roof on Soldier Field, the *Chicago Tribune* published a graphic showing what Daley had in mind. We created a quick 'n' dirty graphic with the same perspective in a 3D program.

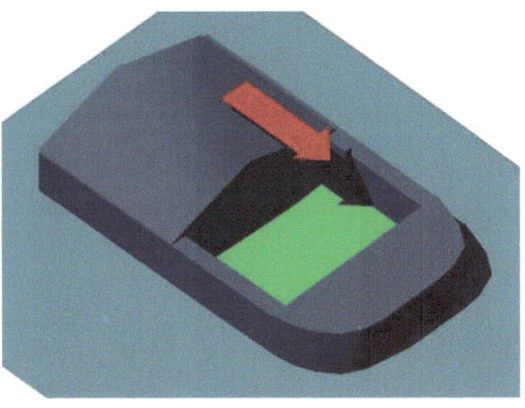

*Graphics like this can be created more quickly in 3D software.*

High quality rendering can give even simple graphics like this a classy look.

**More Complex Illustrations**—The next step up is single objects that are more carefully crafted and more detailed, often rendered with textures, shadows, reflections and depth of field. You might want to make them photorealistic. Check out the

# 3D IN PRINT

model of the Capitol building on the editorial page layout on page 75.

Let's look at some of the objects you can model using the 3D tools described in previous chapters:

### ■ Products

This is an important use of 3D for print designers. The models can be reused in other positions, and in a variety of media. 3D representations of products have a clear, crisp quality, and they are often less expensive and more dynamic than photos of the product.

### ■ Buildings

You can model buildings from scratch in your 3D application, either with precision or guesswork, or you can import models. Earlier in the chapter, we mentioned 3D scanners and applications that can create 3D models from photographs. Another possibility: Suppose you want to create a model of a fast food restaurant. You can take photos of the sides of the restaurant down the street, import them as textures, create a model the same shape as the restaurant and plaster the textures on sides of the model.

Perhaps you want to depict a proposed building that doesn't exist yet. You can show readers what it will look like. Architects who use CAD or 3D modeling software might supply you with three-dimensional views of the project. If they use a "walkthrough" application, they may be able to show you what it would be like to stroll through the building. Ask them to provide you with screenshots from the walkthrough.

### ■ Human Faces and Figures

The easiest way to incorporate models of human faces and figures into your 3D work is to download from the Internet models saved in a format compatible with your software. (Make sure there are

# 3D IN PRINT

no restrictions on commercial use of the models.) Or, try Poser from SmithMicro (see chapter 3). It comes with models of the human figure that can be posed and clothed.

More adventurous designers might want to model heads or human figures themselves. Tutorials included with your software application and tutorials on the Web should be helpful. You will soon discover: (1) modeling the human figure can be very difficult, and (2) 3D artists tackle the task of modeling human faces and figures in many different ways. (Links to many 3D tutorials can be found at www.3dlinks.com.) Our advice: have fun tackling the project, but if you are running out of time, try Poser or import a model.

## ■ Animals

Models of animals abound in CD collections and on the Internet, but you can create your own version of cats, dogs and dinosaurs if you prefer. Applications that include fur and hair capabilities come in particularly handy here.

## ■ Photorealistic Scenes

Three-dimensional scenes can bring a story to life. 3D software is uniquely suited for creating dozens of models and giving the entire scene a photorealistic quality.

If the scene is a landscape, it might be created more easily in a terrain-building application such as Bryce 3D or World Construction Set.

## ■ Large Scale Projects

You are in the big leagues when you use 3D for major projects like these . . .

■ 3D-oriented software played a big role in the design of the 90-story Eureka Tower in Melbourne, Australia—the tallest residential building in the world.

# 3D IN PRINT

■ A downloadable PDF paper on the web describes "The Design and Development of a Virtual 3D City Model". Illustrations show several 3D city projects including Virtual Los Angeles, New York, Zurich, Tokyo and Bologna, Italy. Then, the research team responsible for the paper describes the steps it took to develop its own 3D city model, which it called Shah Alam Virtual City. The paper may be found at www.hitl.washington. edu/people/bdc/virtualcities.pdf

■ A few years ago, a design consortium used AutoCAD applications to design and promote the $16 billion Hong Kong airport project. *Computer Graphics World* reported government officials used the video to convince taxpayers and industrialists to support the project. Computer generated artwork depicted dynamic views of the interior of the terminal, the Hong Kong skyline, and a new rail system that was planned as part of the airport.

■ A consortium of companies and organizations led by the American Institute of Architects undertook the task of creating a massive, detailed virtual model of Philadelphia.

## ■ Infographics

Newspapers, magazines and newsletters make heavy use of infographics for communicating information. Readers often grasp such information more readily if it is incorporated into graphics than they would if it were explained in news or feature articles. *USA Today* makes excellent use of color infographics, ranging from small graphics to full-page illustrations. An example of a large infographic is on page 89.

## LARGEST TRUCKING COMPANIES IN THE U.S.
### (Total revenue)

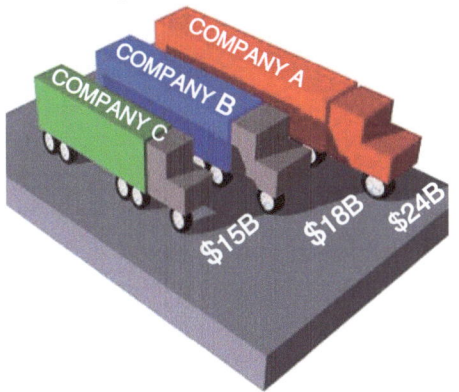

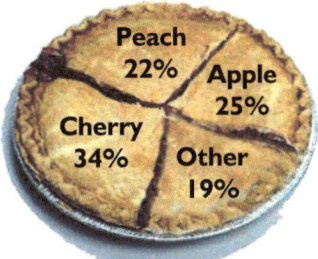

**PIE LOVERS' FAVORITES**

*A real pie chart.*

You can use basic 3D software to create info-graphics. Also available are specialized software applications capable of creating 3D charts and graphs from precise data. Be sure the charting or graphing process does not distort the data by exaggerating differences.

## ■ 3D Representation / Analysis of Data

The use of 3D graphics to represent data from real-world projects is becoming increasingly common. Information on medical conditions is easier to grasp when it is viewed as 3D representations of the human body. 3D visualization of oil field data makes it easier to see locations where hidden oil deposits might lie. *Computer Graphics World* reported that Goodyear Tire & Rubber Co. translated vehicle data into a 4D visualization for analysis of a car's performance and the effects on the car's tires.

# 3D IN PRINT

## ■ Cropping 2D Art for 3D Effect

It isn't always necessary to use a 3D application to produce dramatic 3D effects. If your 2D artwork lends itself to 3D presentation, you can create dramatic layouts by cropping photos creatively. (See the layout section beginning on page 99.)

## ■ Headlines and Logos

3D type can be dynamic whether it stands alone or is part of a 3D scene.

One way of creating a 3D logo easily is to import a 2D version of the logo into a 3D application in a format which the application accepts and then extrude it.

Most of the time you will create headlines and logos as you work in your 3D software or in specialized 3D font applications. Which brings us to the next chapter . . .

# CHAPTER 5

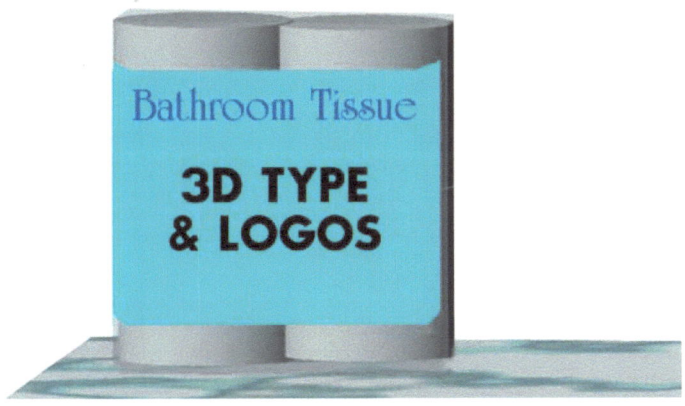

*T*ype used for chunks of text usually is plain and unexceptional. It doesn't need to be dynamic because people seeking information or entertainment don't want to be slowed down by the typeface. They simply want the text to be easy to read. In other words, functional.

But print designers often desire compelling and expressive type for nameplates, logos and headlines. So, they rev up a 2D drawing application or page layout program, create a heading and slap a shadow behind it . . .

## Presto! Instant 3D!

Softer shadows add a touch of sophistication . . .

## Entertainment

For a more exciting look, 3D applications can create "real" 3D type by extrusion . . .

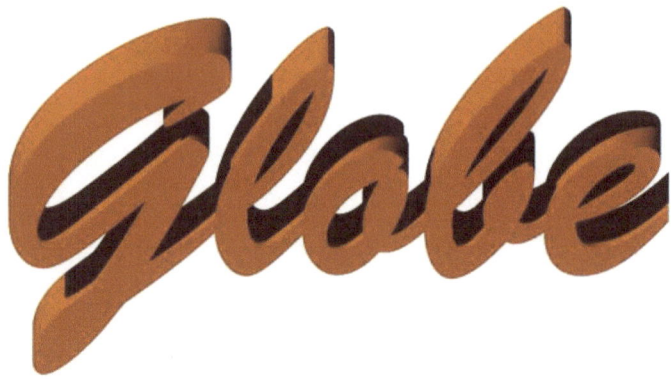

Lighting can offer welcome relief from the even texture of type, casting shadows . . .

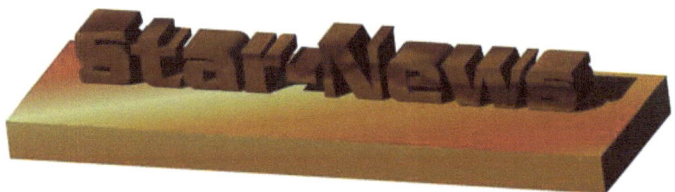

Let's not stop there. How about filled type? Use the "paste into" function in Adobe Illustrator, Adobe Photoshop and similar applications for cool effects. Be sure the artwork you copy fits inside the letters neatly (use big type), and you might want to use a shadow. For an article about sweets, the headline might look like this . . .

## The Terrible Truth About

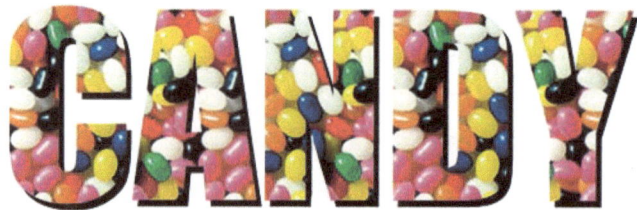

# 3D IN PRINT

Let's tap into textures. Create exciting type in 3D applications by extruding fonts, then applying one of the application's textures to the type. Or import your own textures.

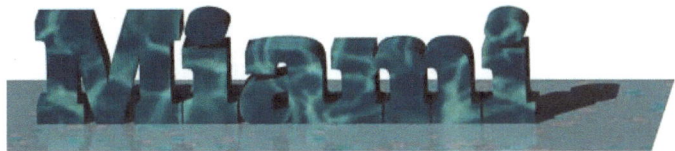

Perhaps you prefer massaged type. TypeStyler, a Macintosh application from Strider Software, can arch, curve, squeeze, or expand type . . .

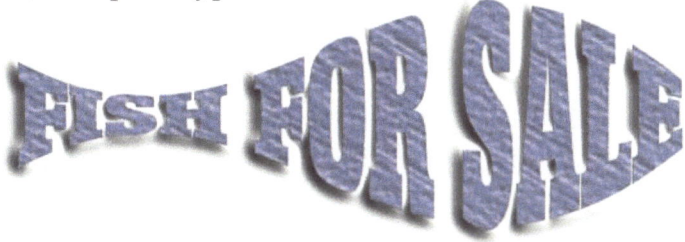

Perspective type is particularly useful for emphasizing a three-dimensional effect . . .

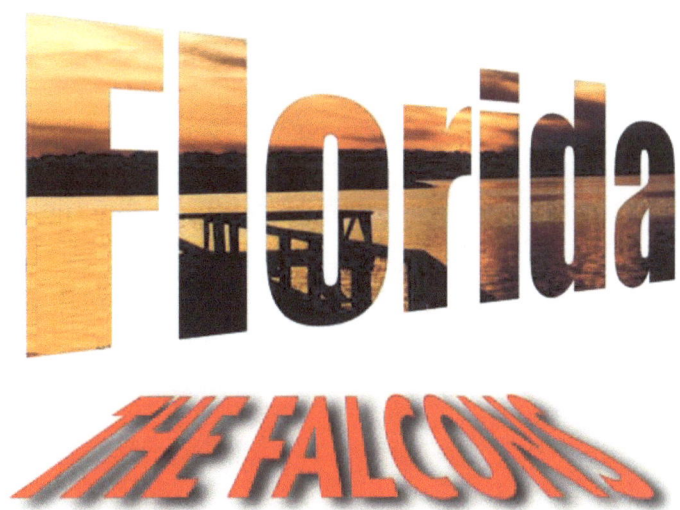

# 3D IN PRINT

Type can be attached to a path in a 2D program . . .

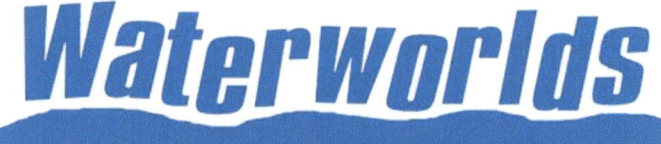

You can also plaster type on 3D objects . . .

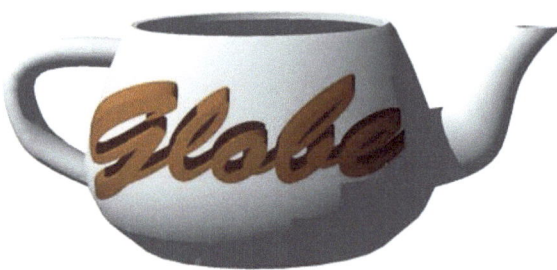

And, if you want to emphasize the three-dimensional nature of the type, you might use a 3D graphic with it . . .

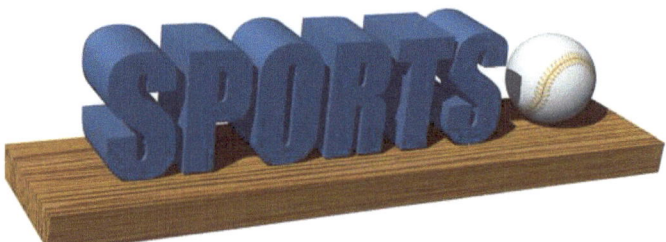

... or merge the type with a photo of an object. (In the example below, the type was manipulated using the polar coordinates filter in Adobe Photoshop.)

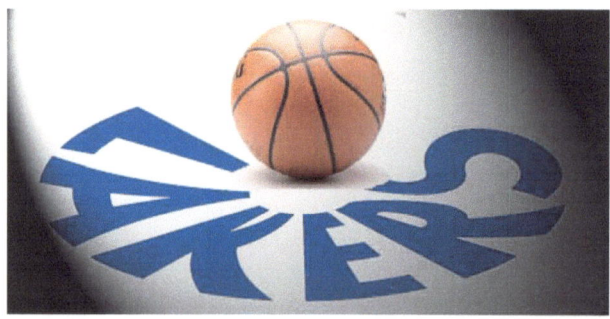

# 3D IN PRINT

## Using 3D Type

Some of the most common uses of 3D type are these:

### ■ Headlines

You might use 3D type for headlines because you want to grab the reader's attention, or you might use it because it is particularly appropriate for the story, such as the jelly bean type on page 52.

### ■ The Publication's Nameplate

The title on the front page of publications has been called, at various times, the flag, nameplate, title, logotype and logo, among other things. The title serves a publication in the same way a logo serves other business enterprises: providing a unique identity. The logo might consist only of the name of the publication . . .

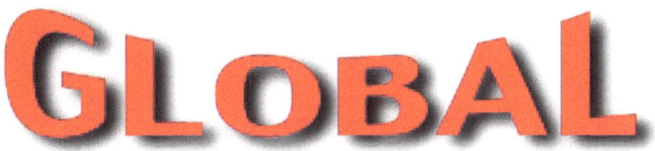

. . . or graphics might be incorporated into the nameplate . . .

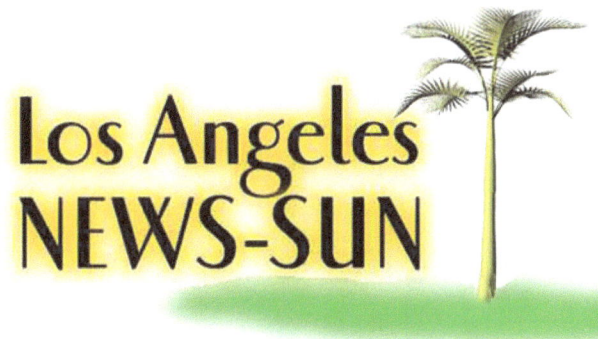

# 3D IN PRINT

Television networks have pioneered a third, more dynamic type of logo. Large extruded type occupies center stage, bathed in light from spotlights. And the name is animated. This type of logo is typically used for movies of the week and prime-time news shows, such as "Dateline NBC" and "20/20'.

Would a logo as spectacular as this be appropriate for a print publication? Perhaps. But newspapers, magazines and newsletters are wisely reluctant to adopt extravagant forms of logos because they risk damaging their relationship with readers, their reputation for serious reporting and their ties to their publication's past. Besides, glittering 3D logos would dominate the page, detracting from story content. And they often would be difficult to merge into cover or front page layouts.

Even so, ornate logos might be appropriate in some instances. What would they look like? Perhaps like this . . .

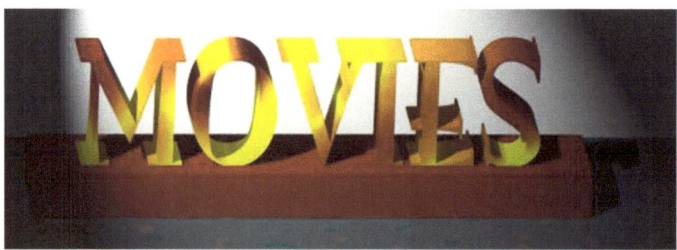

## ■ Headings That Identify a Series of Articles, Special Sections or Events

Standing heads, section headings and headings that tie several articles on the same subject together help organize content for readers. Special headings like these give a series of articles or a section a strong cohesiveness. 3D type is often used for such headings.

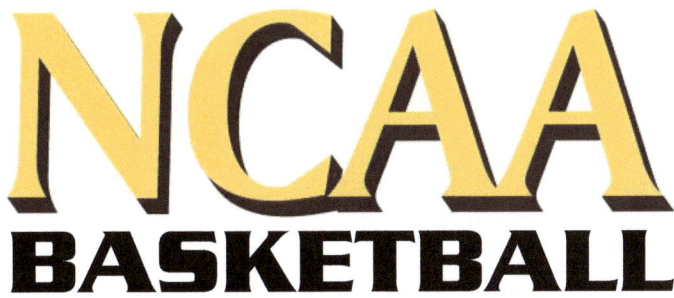

Filled type might be just the ticket for a standing head. A page from a newspaper was used for the texture here . . .

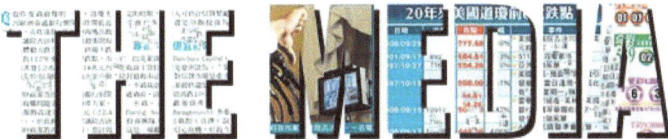

Such filled type might be combined with another element . . .

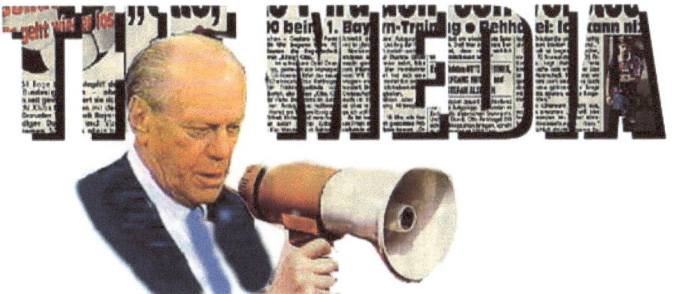

## ■ Type Incorporated Into Artwork

Sometimes type is most effective if it is actually part of the 3D illustration, such as the teapot on page 54 and the basketball scene on page 58.

# 3D IN PRINT

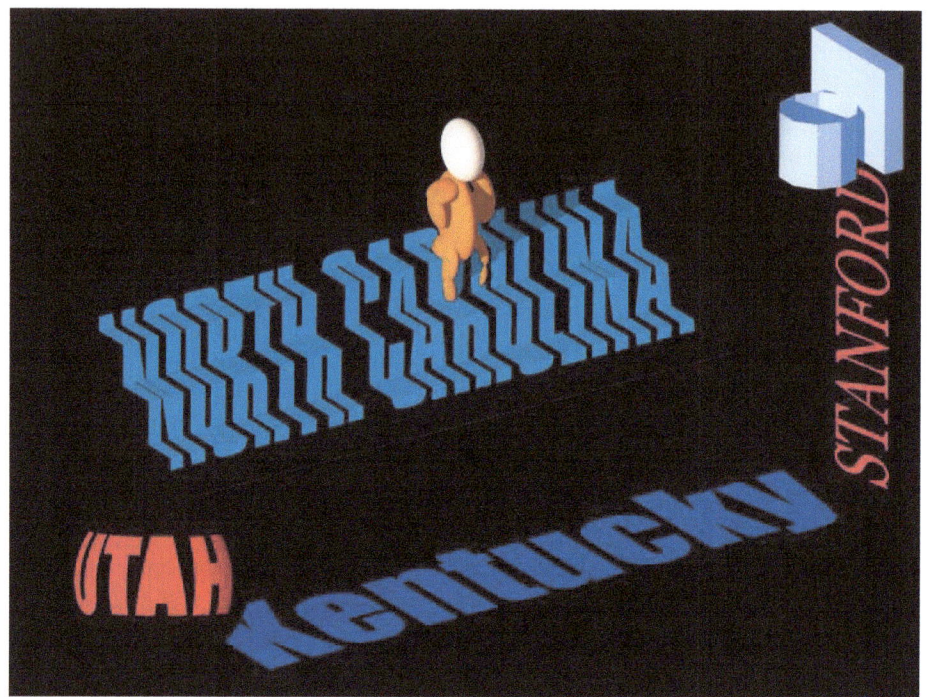

Or, type can be incorporated into a photograph . . ..

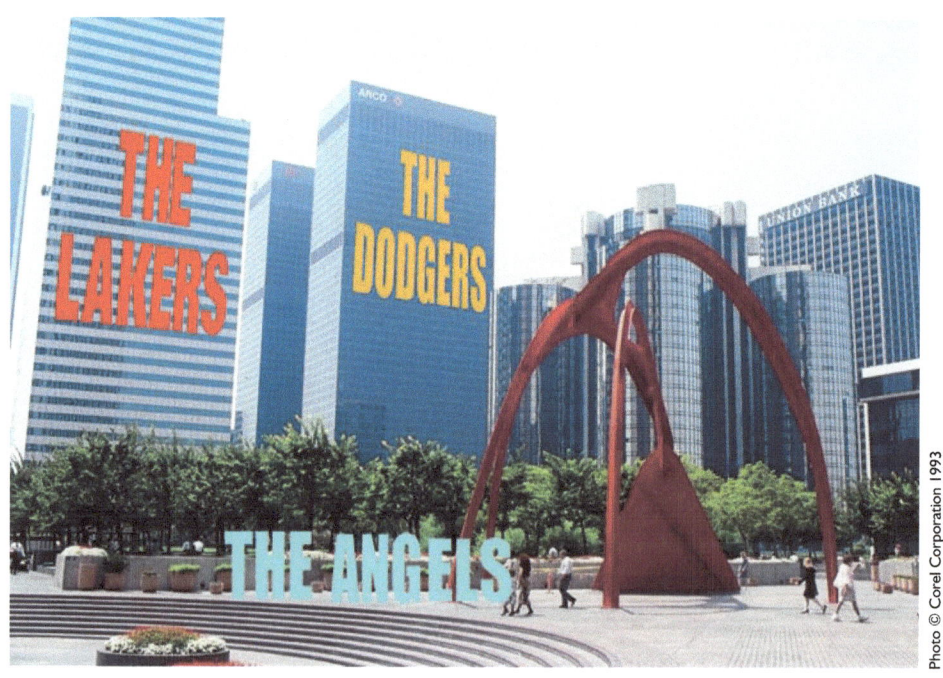

# 3D IN PRINT

    The bottom line is this: creative use of type can be exciting and effective, but the designer must show restraint in the use of 3D type, avoiding silliness and excess.

# CHAPTER 6

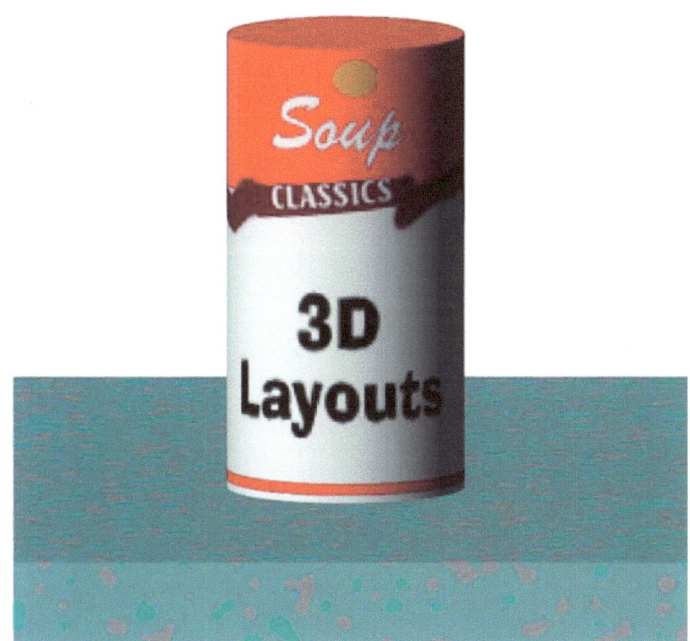

**P**lastered on a printed page, photographs and 3D elements often seem to have the depth squeezed out of them. There are ways to give printed pages a three dimensional look, however.

First, we will look at creating 3D layouts that fall into these categories:

### Pages With Photos as the Dominant Element

- Cropped and scaled photos
- Photos manipulated in image retouching applications

### Pages With 3D Graphics as the Dominant Element

- 3D graphic in a 2D layout
- The layout as a 3D graphic

### Arranging Graphics, Headlines and Text for 3D Effect

- Building a 3D page
- "Comin' at you" layouts
- Setting up layouts in a 3D program
- Using a 3D box for layouts

# 3D IN PRINT

The last part of this chapter consists of page layouts that embody many of these ideas.

3D layouts—like most other page layouts—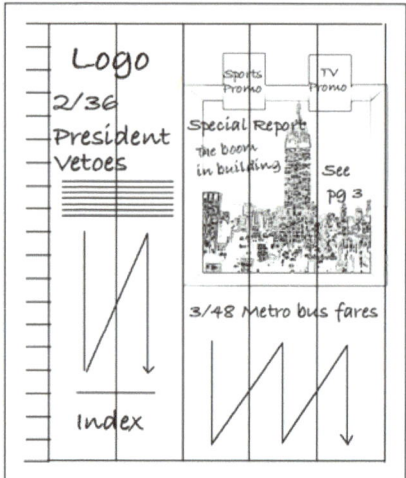 can be worked out on paper before a layout is attempted on a computer. Give expression to your ideas and flights of fancy without worrying about how to implement them. If you know what you want to accomplish, you will waste less time and work more purposefully on the computer.

On the other hand, if you do some of your layouts on the computer, you might stumble across exciting ideas while exploring your 3D application's capabilities.

## Pages With Photos as the Dominant Element

You can create 3D pages without using graphics created in 3D applications. Simply take a striking photograph and crop, scale or manipulate it to give your pages a 3D look.

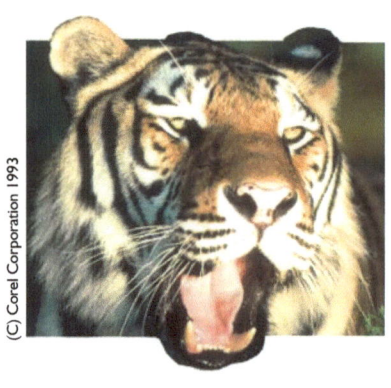

### ■ Cropped and Scaled Photos

As mentioned in chapter 4, one way to show depth is creative cropping of a 2D photo or 3D graphic. Take the artwork into a photo retouching application and see what you can do by cropping (see pages 99, 100, 103 and 105) or by scaling (page 113, where the Russian towers over the Russian scene).

# 3D IN PRINT

## ■ Photos Manipulated in Image Retouching Applications

You can do more than merely crop or scale photographs to give them a 3D appearance. Try out the embossing filter and other filters in applications like Photoshop. And special 3D filters for Photoshop provide an easy way to simulate 3D graphics.

## Pages With 3D Graphics as the Dominant Element

Manipulating photos is helpful, but your arsenal of weapons for 3D layouts expands greatly when you have at your disposal graphics created in 3D applications.

### ■ 3D Graphic in a 2D Layout

Many times, a layout will consist only of a dominant 3D graphic and the usual two dimensional elements, such as headlines and body type. The layout is basically 2D, but the graphic is unmistakably 3D. Below is an example of a 3D graphic that dominates a layout which is otherwise 2D.

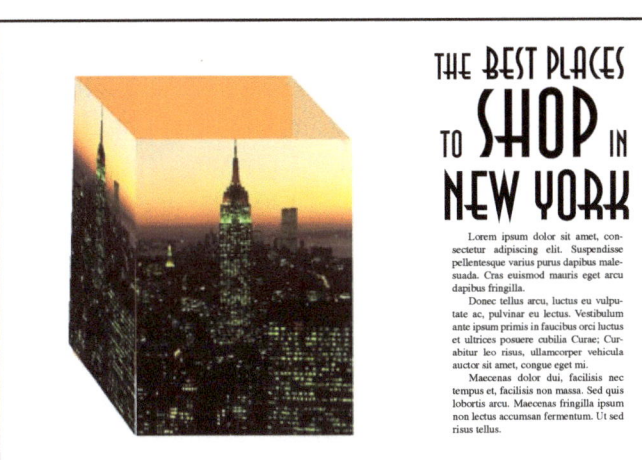

THE BEST PLACES TO SHOP IN NEW YORK

Lorem ipsum dolor sit amet, consectetur adipiscing elit. Suspendisse pellentesque varius purus dapibus malesuada. Cras euismod mauris eget arcu dapibus fringilla.

Donec tellus arcu, luctus eu vulputate ac, pulvinar eu lectus. Vestibulum ante ipsum primis in faucibus orci luctus et ultrices posuere cubilia Curae; Curabitur leo risus, ullamcorper vehicula auctor sit amet, congue eget mi.

Maecenas dolor dui, facilisis nec tempus et, facilisis non massa. Sed quis lobortis arcu. Maecenas fringilla ipsum non lectus accumsan fermentum. Ut sed risus tellus.

NYC photo © Corel Corporation 1993

# 3D IN PRINT

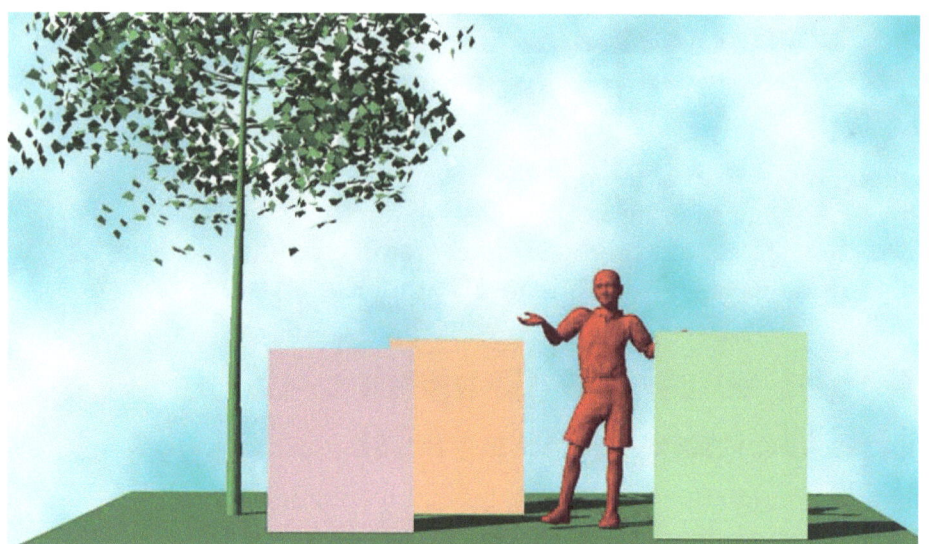

### ■ The Layout as a 3D Graphic

At times, you might want to make the headline and body type part of the 3D graphic. The entire layout becomes a 3D scene. For example, headlines easily can be added to the graphic above (see page 115 for the finished layout.)

## Arranging Elements on the Page for a 3D Effect

The layout methods we have discussed so far are based on the use of a dominant piece of artwork, either a photograph or a 3D graphic. But the print designer can take a more active role, arranging several elements on the page in a way that gives it a strong 3D look.

### ■ Building a 3D Page

Fascinating pages can be built if the designer arranges the 2D and 3D elements in a story/layout package in a way that emphasizes perspective.

# 3D IN PRINT

When the designer arranges art and story in this way, there are many factors to consider. For example . . .

- Individual elements of the package are interrelated. Each element has the correct perspective and scaling in relation to the other elements.
- If there is more than one 3D element, shadows should fall correctly on all the elements, depending on the location of the light source(s).
- Type is an integral part of the whole, not a separate entity. It is proportionally sized and logically placed in relation to other elements of the package.

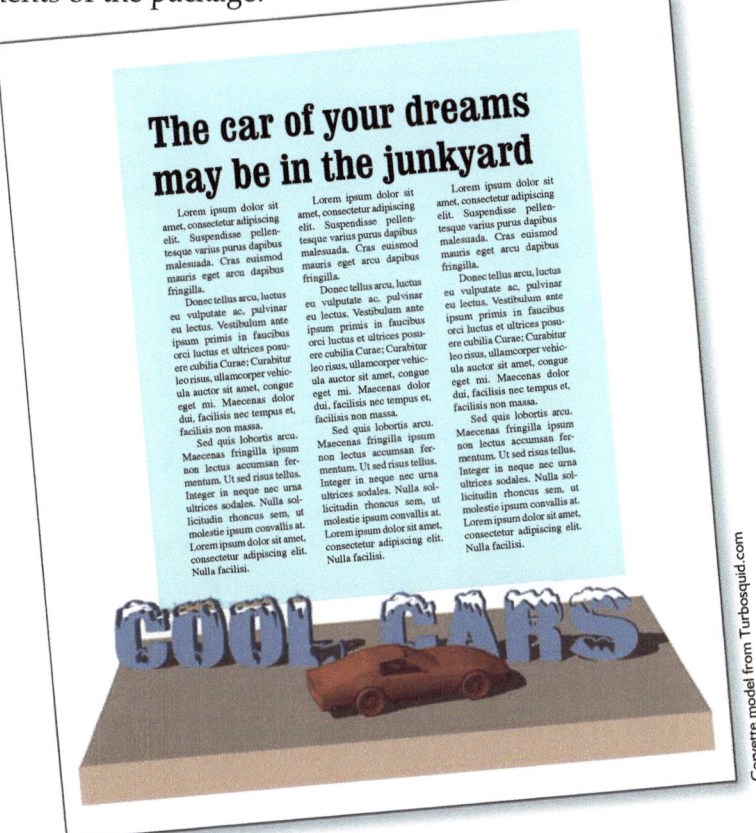

Corvette model from Turbosquid.com

# 3D IN PRINT

■ When appropriate, depth of field can be used, with some objects less distinct than other objects.

■ The entire single page or double-page layout is a unit.

■ Overlapping of text and graphic elements sometimes leads to a more harmonious, integrated layout.

■ Headline and body type often are reversed into 3D graphics—but if you want the type to be read, it must be legible.

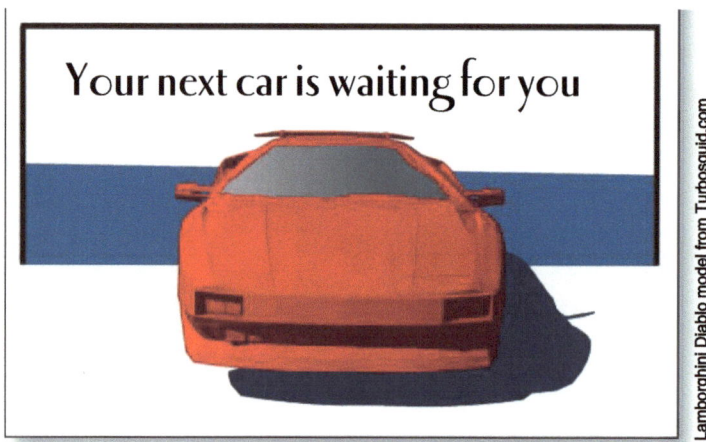

Your next car is waiting for you

Lamborghini Diablo model from Turbosquid.com

### ■ "Comin' at You" Layouts

Another way of arranging elements for 3D effects is the "comin' at you" approach. You can create graphics that seem to jump off the screen—or the printed page. At the movies, silly looking glasses with red and blue lenses for 3D have been making a comeback. When actors or cartoon characters throw objects at the camera, the objects seem to leap into the theater. Print designers can achieve a similar effect using perspective and depth of field—either through artwork or layout.

# 3D IN PRINT

By incorporating "comin' at you" graphics into your layouts and playing them big, the entire page can have an eye-popping 3D look. See the layouts on pages 121 and 124.

## ■ Setting Up Layouts in a 3D Program

Sometimes it is possible to construct a 3D layout in a 3D application. There are advantages:

■ All elements will have the proper perspective, scaling and shadows—including elements that will contain type.

■ If the software supports depth of field, all elements also will have the proper depth of field.

■ If the light source illuminates the scene from a central point, shadows on

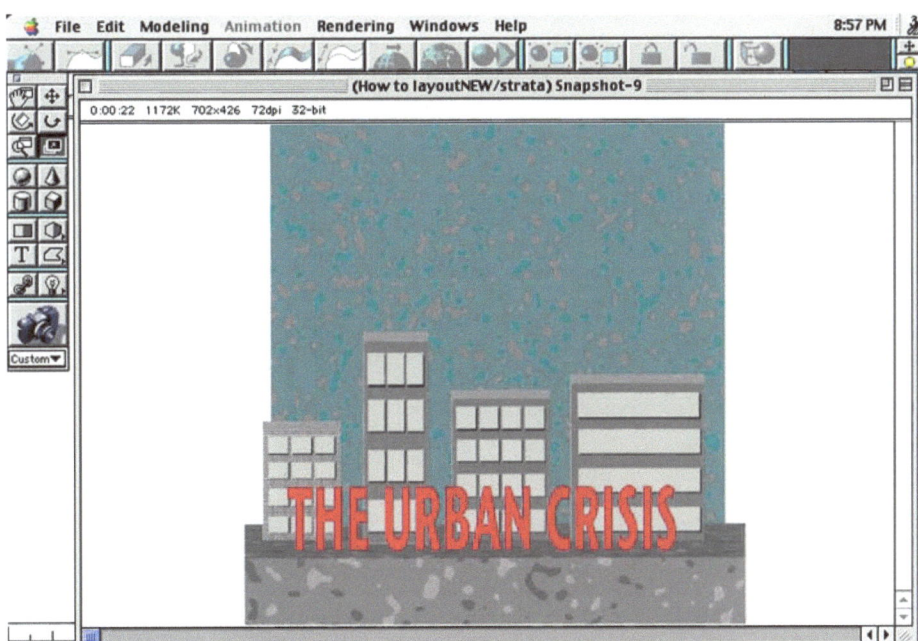

*Creating a layout in a 3D application. This screenshot shows headline type, 3D artwork and a placeholder for body type (the "wall" in back). Text will be added later.*

# 3D IN PRINT

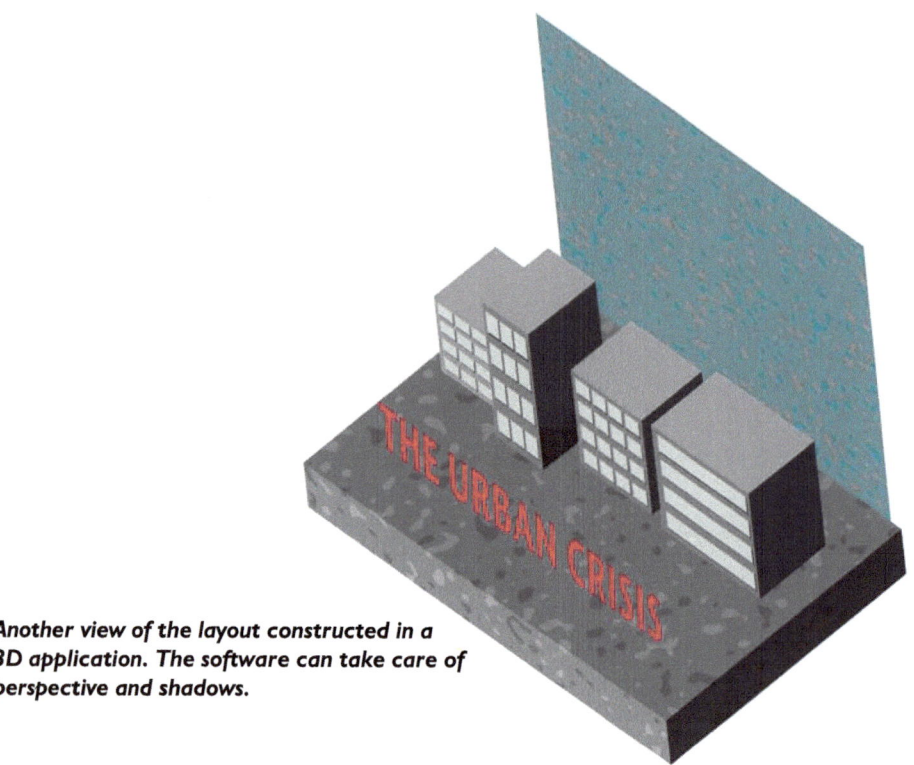

*Another view of the layout constructed in a 3D application. The software can take care of perspective and shadows.*

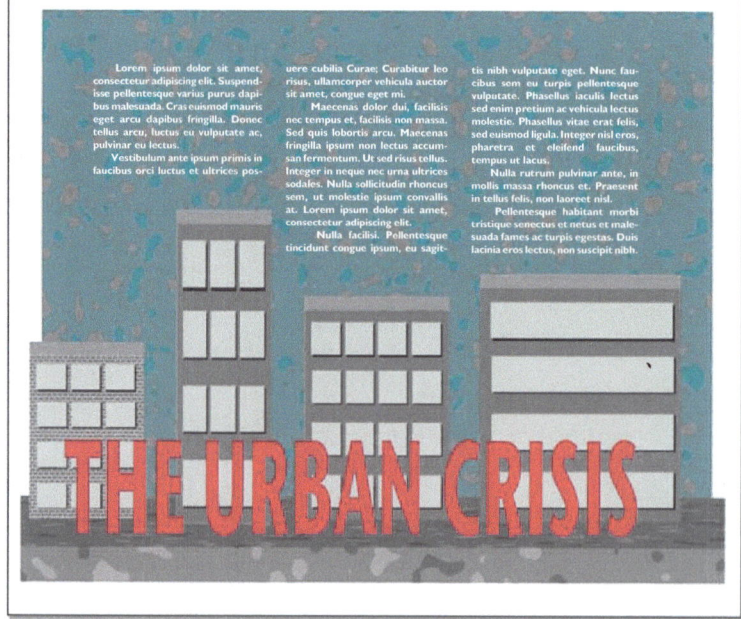

*The final magazine spread for the layout created in the 3D application might look like this.*

# 3D IN PRINT

layout elements will fall in different directions, depending on where they are located. If a single light source is off to the side, all shadows will fall in the same direction.

Headlines can be placed in the actual 3D scene if desired, but normally you will want to set up a placeholder for body copy. This is desirable because smaller type might be blurry or unreadable if it is rendered with the scene, particularly if depth of field is applied. And if revisions are made in body copy, as is often the case, the changes can be made much more easily if body type is added later when the 3D artwork is placed into a page layout program such as Quark XPress or Adobe's InDesign or Page-Maker.

If body type needs to be slipped partially behind another element, we can combine the text and layout in a program such as Adobe Photoshop and touch up the layout.

## ■ Using a 3D Box for Layouts

You can create a 3D box in an application and use it to add perspective to your layouts. It's a simple idea, but it can produce stunning layouts.

For example, the box for the page design at the right was set up in a 3D application. Then, a few details were added in Photoshop and type and headlines were placed on the layout in InDesign. The final page layout appears on page 96.

Other examples are on pages 93, 94 and 95. And don't miss the sports page layout on page 83.

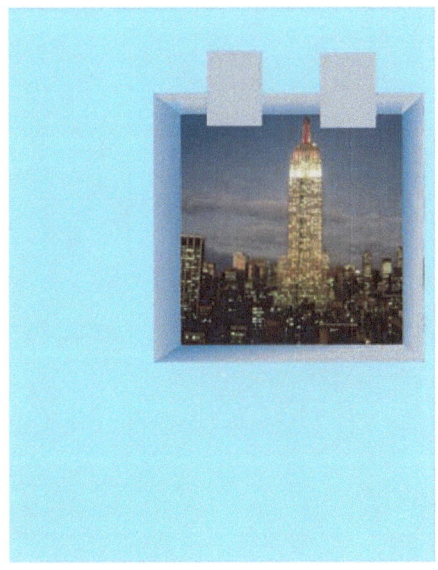

Photo © Corel Corporation 1993

# 3D IN PRINT

The book page (page 97) is a variation of this idea. Instead of using a box, a shelf is placed in front of the text to provide a sense of depth.

## Fuel for Your Creativity

On the following pages are rough layouts. They illustrate some of the ways three-dimensional design can be effectively implemented in print publications. Although each example was prepared specifically for one medium—newspaper, magazine, newsletter, print advertising, brochures, book covers or posters—the ideas apply to the other media as well

Incidentally, don't strain your eyes trying to read the text of stories—it's dummy type.

# Examples of 3D Layouts

# Pages Built Around 3D Models

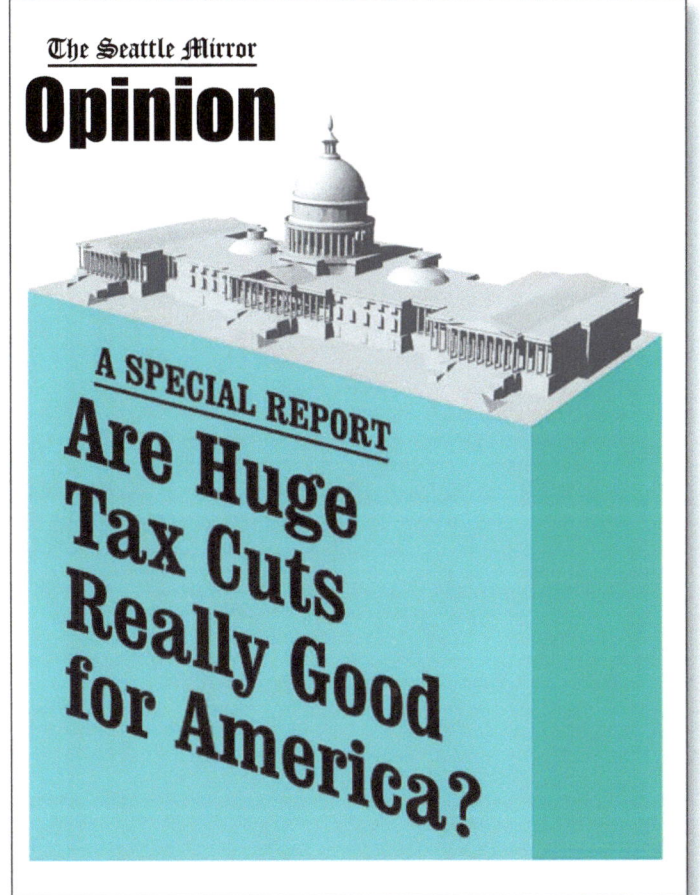

Capitol model: 3D Cafe /Platinum Pictures Multimedia Inc.

*Placing the Capitol Building on top of a block gives the page a dramatic 3D effect. Type can be added in the 3D application, Photoshop, or the page design software.*

# 3D IN PRINT

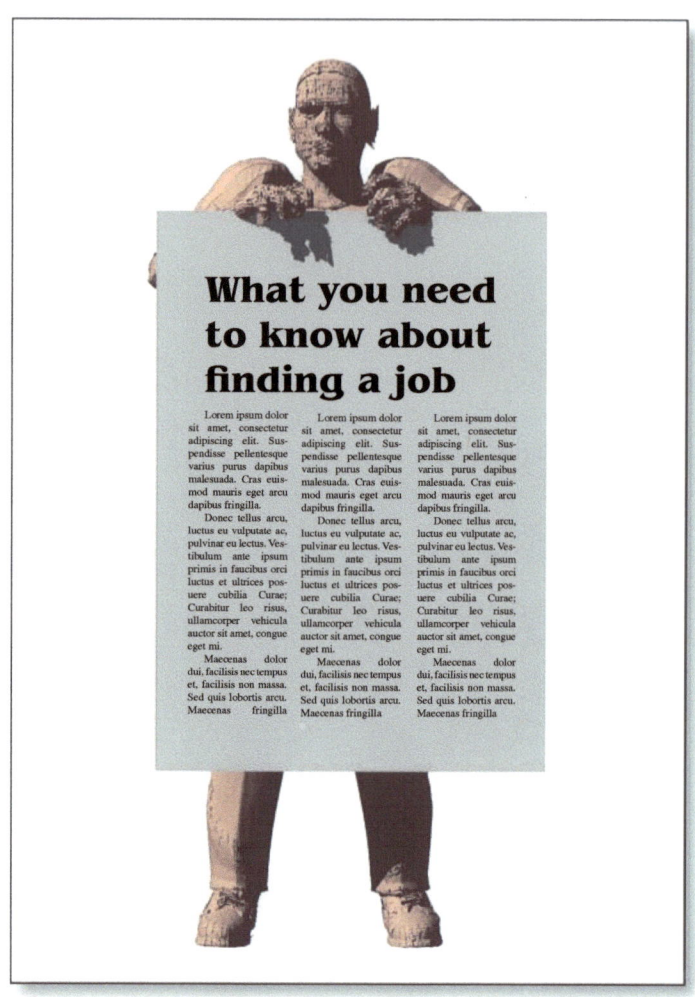

*This page has entered the third dimension in a dramatic way.*

# 3D IN PRINT

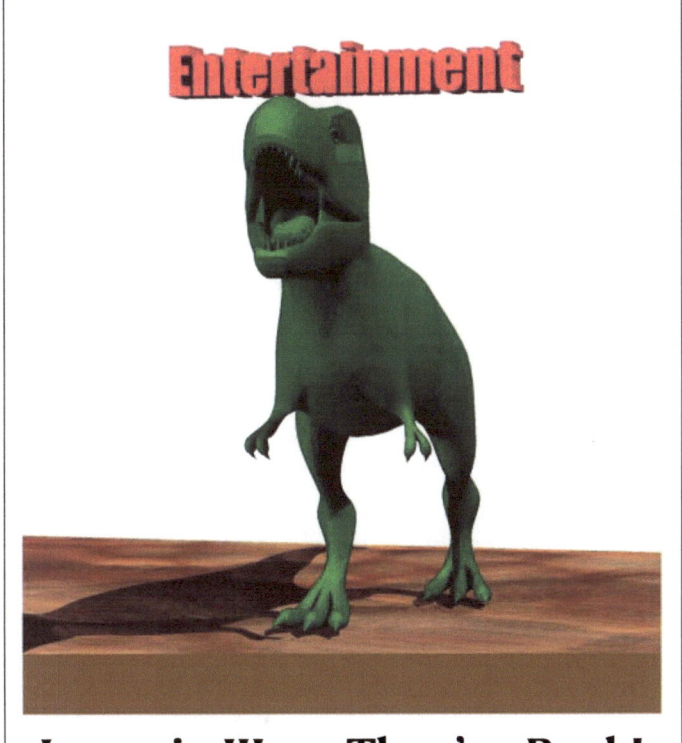

## Entertainment

## Jurassic III — They're Back!

Lorem ipsum dolor sit amet, consbr adipiscing elit. Suspendisse pellentesque varius purus dapibus malesuada. Cras euismod mauris eget arcu dapibus fringilla.

Donec tellus arcu, luctus eu vulputate ac, pulvinar eu lectus. Vestibulum ante ipsum primis in faucibus orci luctus et ultrices posuere cubilia Curae; Curabitur leo risus, ullamcorper vehicula auctor sit amet, congue eget mi. Maecenas dolor dui, facilisis nec tempus et, facilisis non massa.

Lorem ipsum dolor sit amet, consbr adipiscing elit. Suspendisse pellentesque varius purus dapibus malesuada. Cras euismod mauris eget arcu dapibus fringilla.

Donec tellus arcu, luctus eu vulputate ac, pulvinar eu lectus. Vestibulum ante ipsum primis in faucibus orci luctus et ultrices posuere cubilia Curae; Curabitur leo risus, ullamcorper vehicula auctor sit amet, congue eget mi. Maecenas dolor dui, facilisis nec tempus et, facilisis non massa.

Lorem ipsum dolor sit amet, consbr adipiscing elit. Suspendisse pellentesque varius purus dapibus malesuada. Cras euismod mauris eget arcu dapibus fringilla.

Donec tellus arcu, luctus eu vulputate ac, pulvinar eu lectus. Vestibulum ante ipsum primis in faucibus orci luctus et ultrices posuere cubilia Curae; Curabitur leo risus, ullamcorper vehicula auctor sit amet, congue eget mi. Maecenas dolor dui, facilisis nec tempus et, facilisis non massa.

Tyrannosaurus model from Turbosquid.com

*It's less confusing to readers if clues tell them what is in front and what is in back. The reptile overlaps the Entertainment logo, and the floor has a front edge, suggesting body type and headline are in line with the front edge.*

# 3D IN PRINT

## Houston's growth brings new emphasis on limits

Lorem ipsum dolor sit amet, consectetur adipiscing elit. Suspendisse pellentesque varius purus dapibus malesuada. Cras euismod mauris eget arcu dapibus fringilla.

Donec tellus arcu, luctus eu vulputate ac, pulvinar eu lectus. Vestibulum ante ipsum primis in faucibus orci luctus et ultrices posuere cubilia Curae; Curabitur leo risus, ullamcorper vehicula auctor sit amet, congue eget mi. Maecenas dolor dui, facilisis nec tempus et, facilisis non massa.

Sed quis lobortis arcu. Maecenas fringilla ipsum non lectus accumsan fermentum. Ut sed risus tellus. Integer in neque nec urna ultrices sodales. Nulla sollicitudin rhoncus sem, ut molestie ipsum convallis at. Lorem ipsum dolor sit amet, consectetur adipiscing elit. Nulla facilisi.

Pellentesque tincidunt congue ipsum, eu sagittis nibh vulputate eget. Nunc faucibus sem eu turpis pellentesque vulputate. Phasellus iaculis

Lorem ipsum dolor sit amet, consectetur adipiscing elit. Suspendisse pellentesque varius purus dapibus malesuada. Cras euismod mauris eget arcu dapibus fringilla.

Donec tellus arcu, luctus eu vulputate ac, pulvinar eu lectus. Vestibulum ante ipsum primis in faucibus orci luctus et ultrices posuere cubilia Curae; Curabitur leo risus, ullamcorper vehicula auctor sit amet, congue eget mi. Maecenas dolor dui, facilisis nec tempus et, facilisis non massa.

Sed quis lobortis arcu. Maecenas fringilla ipsum non lectus accumsan fermentum. Ut sed risus tellus. Integer in neque nec urna ultrices sodales. Nulla sollicitudin rhoncus sem, ut molestie ipsum convallis at. Lorem ipsum dolor sit amet, consectetur adipiscing elit. Nulla facilisi.

Pellentesque tincidunt congue ipsum, eu sagittis nibh vulputate eget. Nunc faucibus sem eu turpis pellentesque vulputate. Phasellus iaculis

Lorem ipsum dolor sit amet, consectetur adipiscing elit. Suspendisse pellentesque varius purus dapibus malesuada. Cras euismod mauris eget arcu dapibus fringilla.

Donec tellus arcu, luctus eu vulputate ac, pulvinar eu lectus. Vestibulum ante ipsum primis in faucibus orci luctus et ultrices posuere cubilia Curae; Curabitur leo risus, ullamcorper vehicula auctor sit amet, congue eget mi. Maecenas dolor dui, facilisis nec tempus et, facilisis non massa.

Sed quis lobortis arcu. Maecenas fringilla ipsum non lectus accumsan fermentum. Ut sed risus tellus. Integer in neque nec urna ultrices sodales. Nulla sollicitudin rhoncus sem, ut molestie ipsum convallis at. Lorem ipsum dolor sit amet, consectetur adipiscing elit. Nulla facilisi.

Pellentesque tincidunt congue ipsum, eu sagittis nibh vulputate eget. Nunc faucibus sem eu turpis pellentesque vulputate. Phasellus iaculis

Lorem ipsum dolor sit amet, consectetur adipiscing elit. Suspendisse pellentesque varius purus dapibus malesuada. Cras euismod mauris eget arcu dapibus fringilla.

Donec tellus arcu, luctus eu vulputate ac, pulvinar eu lectus. Vestibulum ante ipsum primis in faucibus orci luctus et ultrices posuere cubilia Curae; Curabitur leo risus, ullamcorper vehicula auctor sit amet, congue eget mi. Maecenas dolor dui, facilisis nec tempus et, facilisis non massa.

Sed quis lobortis arcu. Maecenas fringilla ipsum non lectus accumsan fermentum. Ut sed risus tellus. Integer in neque nec urna ultrices sodales. Nulla sollicitudin rhoncus sem, ut molestie ipsum convallis at. Lorem ipsum dolor sit amet, consectetur adipiscing elit. Nulla facilisi.

Pellentesque tincidunt congue ipsum, eu sagittis nibh vulputate eget. Nunc faucibus sem eu turpis pellentesque vulputate. Phasellus iaculis

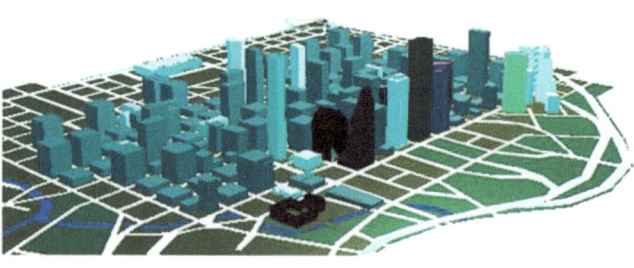

Houston model: 3D Cafe/Platinum Pictures Multimedia Inc.

*Large 3D graphics take more time to create, but they are often worth it. The same model is used on the opposite page.*

# 3D IN PRINT

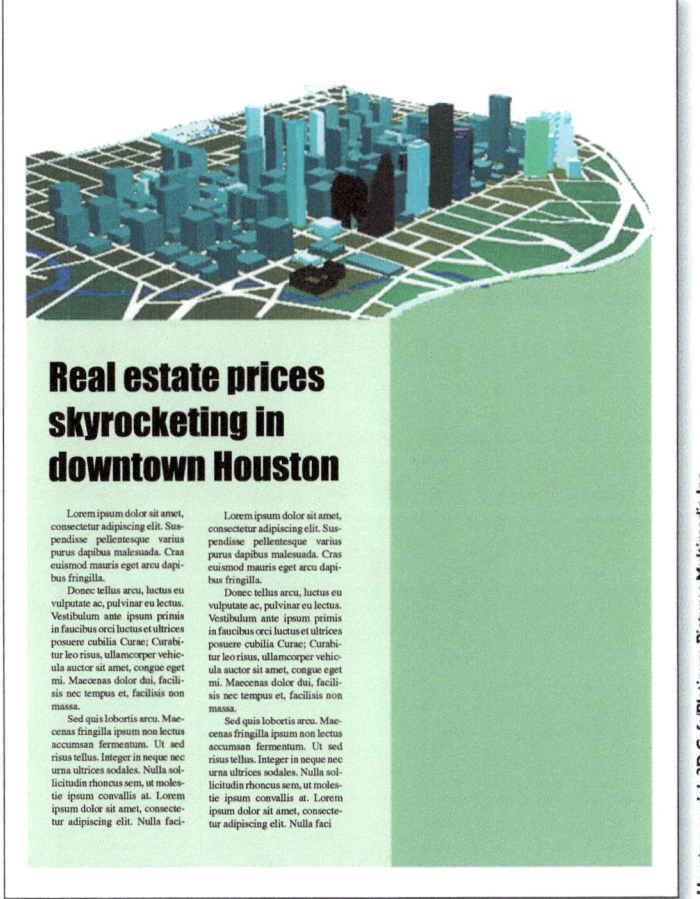

Houston model: 3D Cafe/Platinum Pictures Multimedia Inc.

*Here the model is given an entirely different layout treatment. Both layouts were easy to create.*

# 3D IN PRINT

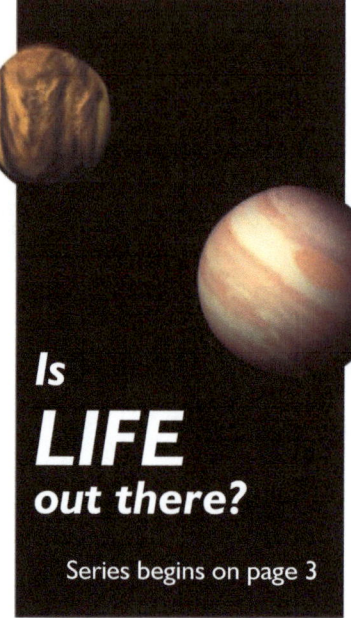

**CINCINNATI NEWS**

## JUDICIAL CONDUCT PROBED

Lorem ipsum dolor sit amet, consectetur adipiscing elit. Suspendisse pellentesque varius purus dapibus malesuada. Cras euismod mauris eget arcu dapibus fringilla.

Donec tellus arcu, luctus eu vulputate ac, pulvinar eu lectus. Vestibulum ante ipsum primis in faucibus orci luctus et ultrices posuere cubilia Curae; Curabitur leo risus, ullamcorper vehicula auctor sit amet, congue eget mi. Maecenas dolor dui, facilisis nec tempus et, facilisis non massa.

Sed quis lobortis arcu. Maecenas fringilla ipsum non lectus accumsan fermentum. Ut sed risus tellus. Integer in neque nec urna ultrices sodales. Nulla sollicitudin rhoncus sem, ut molestie ipsum convallis at. Lorem ipsum dolor sit amet, consectetur adipiscing elit. Nulla facilisi.

Pellentesque tincidunt congue ipsum, eu sagittis nibh vulputate eget. Nunc faucibus sem eu turpis pellentesque vulputate. Phasellus iaculis lectus sed enim pretium ac vehicula

## POLLUTION BILL HEADS FOR HOUSE

Lorem ipsum dolor sit amet, consectetur adipiscing elit. Suspendisse pellentesque varius purus dapibus malesuada. Cras euismod mauris eget arcu dapibus fringilla.

Donec tellus arcu, luctus eu vulputate ac, pulvinar eu lectus. Vestibulum ante ipsum primis in faucibus orci luctus et ultrices posuere cubilia Curae; Curabitur leo risus, ullamcorper vehicula auctor sit amet, congue eget mi. Maecenas dolor dui, facilisis nec tempus et, facilisis non massa.

Sed quis lobortis arcu. Maecenas fringilla ipsum non lectus accumsan fermentum. Ut sed risus tellus. Integer in neque nec urna ultrices sodales. Nulla sollicitudin rhoncus sem, ut molestie ipsum convallis at. Lorem ipsum dolor sit amet, consectetur adipiscing elit. Nulla facilisi.

Pellentesque tincidunt congue ipsum, eu sagittis nibh vulputate eget. Nunc faucibus sem eu turpis pellentesque vulputate. Phasellus iaculis lectus sed enim pretium ac vehicula lectus molestie.

### Is LIFE out there?

Series begins on page 3

## Kentucky Braces for More Tornadoes

Lorem ipsum dolor sit amet, consectetur adipiscing elit. Suspendisse pellentesque varius purus dapibus malesuada. Cras euismod mauris eget arcu dapibus fringilla.

Donec tellus arcu, luctus eu vulputate ac, pulvinar eu lectus. Vestibulum ante ipsum primis in faucibus orci luctus et ultrices posuere cubilia Curae; Curabitur leo risus, ullamcorper vehicula auctor sit amet, congue eget mi. Maecenas dolor dui, facilisis nec tempus et, facilisis non massa.

Sed quis lobortis arcu. Maecenas fringilla

ipsum non lectus accumsan fermentum. Ut sed risus tellus. Integer in neque nec urna ultrices sodales. Nulla sollicitudin rhoncus sem, ut molestie ipsum convallis at. Lorem ipsum dolor sit amet, consectetur adipiscing elit. Nulla facilisi.

Pellentesque tincidunt congue ipsum, eu sagittis nibh vulputate eget. Nunc faucibus sem eu turpis pellentesque vulputate. Phasellus iaculis lectus sed enim pretium ac vehicula lectus molestie.

## ZOO REOPENS TUESDAY

Phasellus vitae erat felis, sed euismod ligula. Integer nisl eros, pharetra et eleifend faucibus, tempus ut lacus. Nulla rutrum pulvinar ante, in mollis massa rhoncus et. Praesent in tellus felis, non laoreet nisl.

Pellentesque habitant morbi tristique senectus et netus et malesuada fames ac turpis egestas. Duis lacinia eros lectus, non suscipit nibh. Mauris nulla est, ultrices sed vulputate sit

*The way you use graphics can make a page stand out.*

# 3D IN PRINT

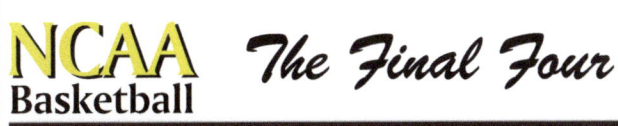

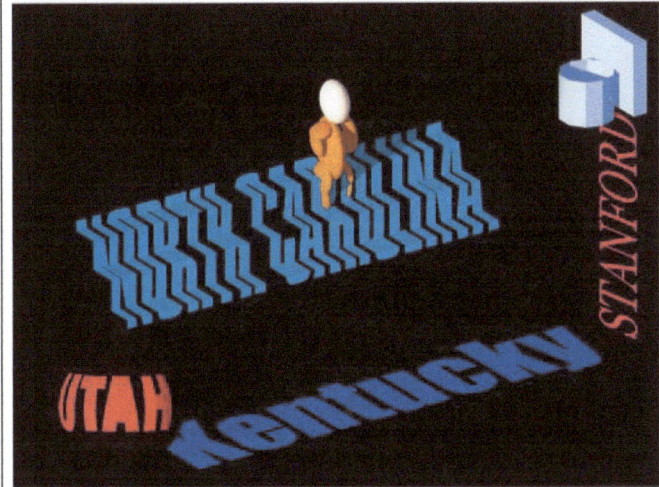

*Type can be an integral part of a 3D graphic. The lighting and black background helped make the graphic effective.*

# Arranging Elements for a 3D Effect

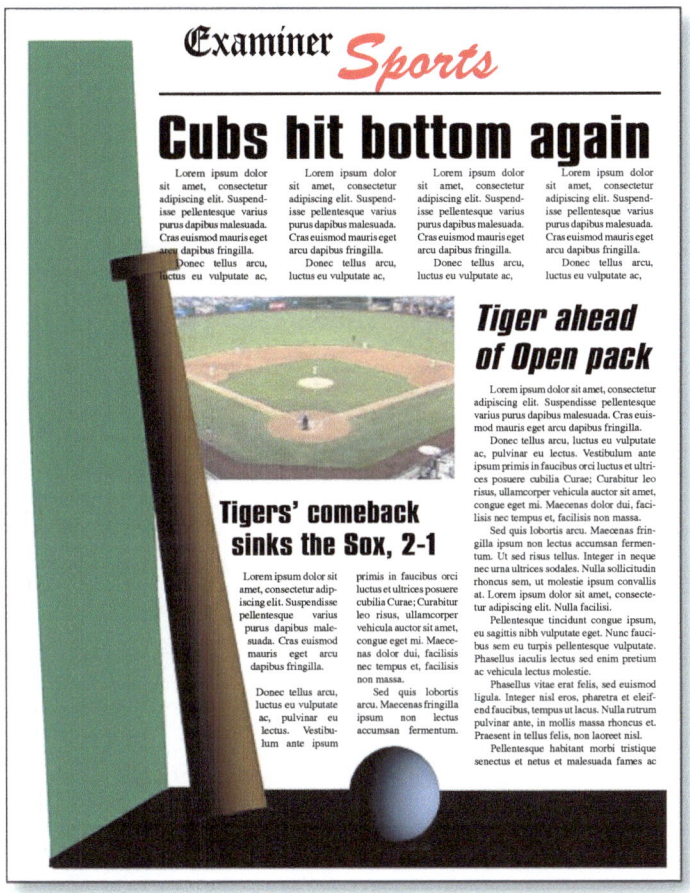

*An eye-catching layout. The ball, bat and side panels can be created easily in a 3D application.*

# 3D IN PRINT

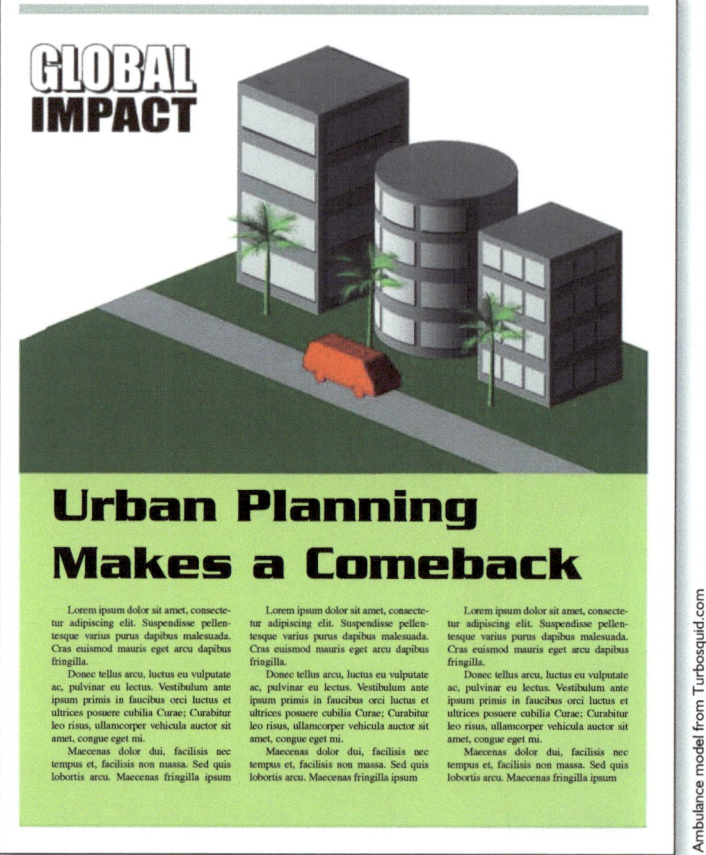

*3D graphics can give your pages depth and perspective. Most photographs do not.*

# 3D IN PRINT

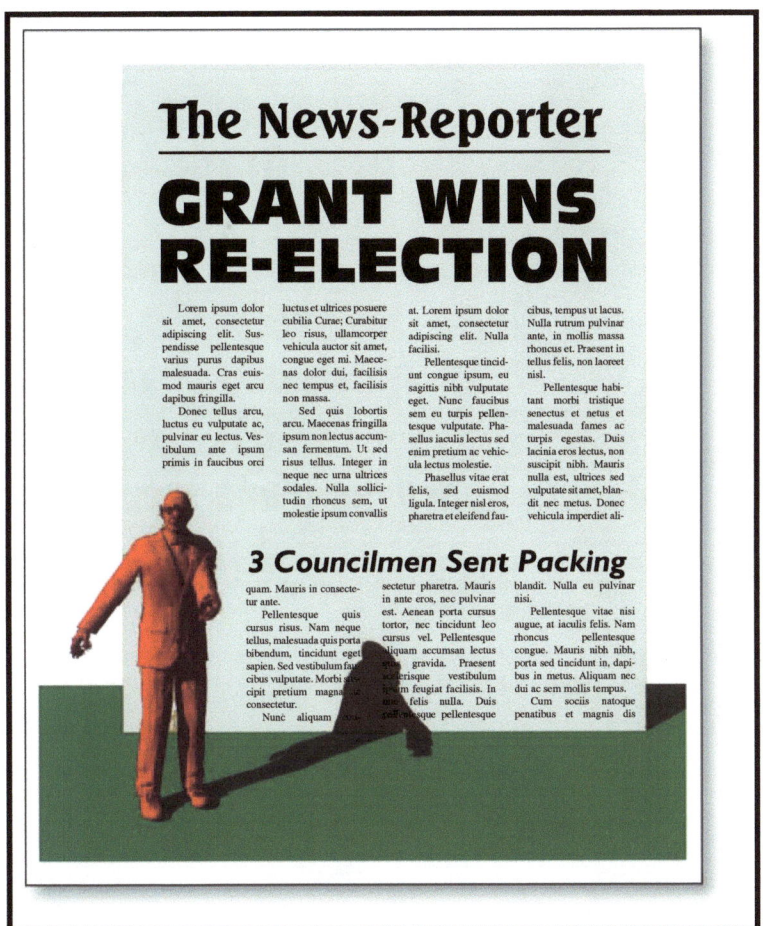

*The winner stands out in this example of election coverage. The shadow falling on the newspaper is a nice touch.*

# 3D IN PRINT

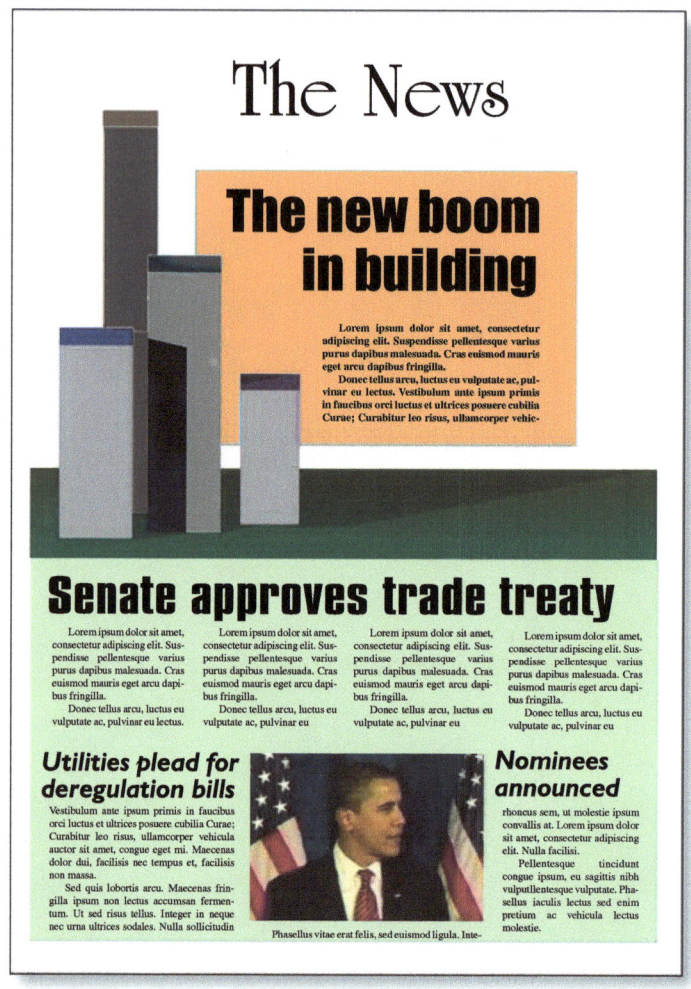

*The buildiings could be texture-mapped with photos of actual skyscraper surfaces. The stories on the bottom half of the page are clearly in front of the 3D graphic—not behind it.*

# 3D IN PRINT

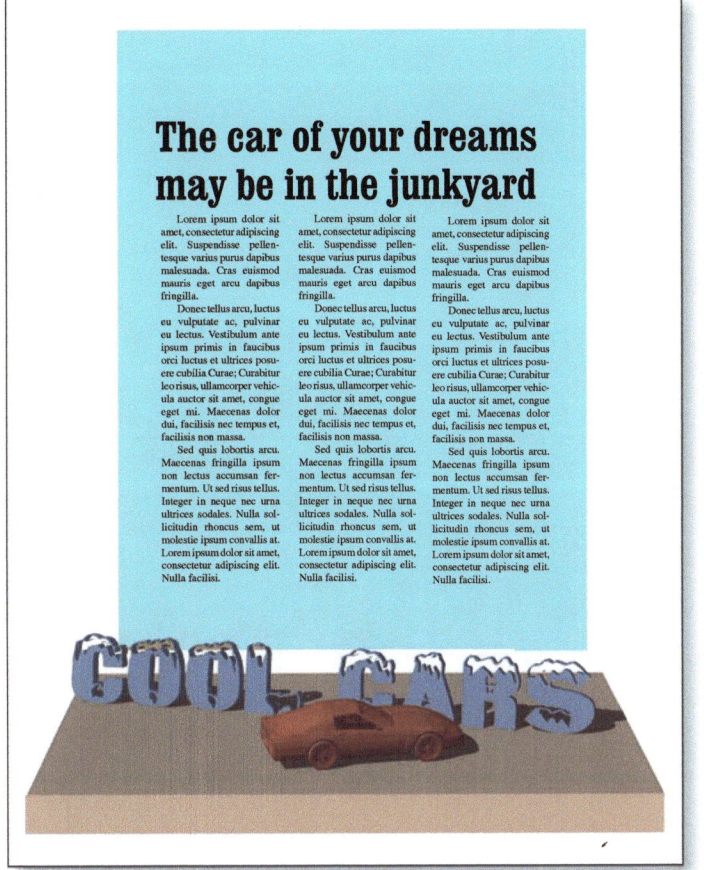

Corvette model from Turbosquid.com

*3D type and a model of a car give the page impact.*

# 3D IN PRINT

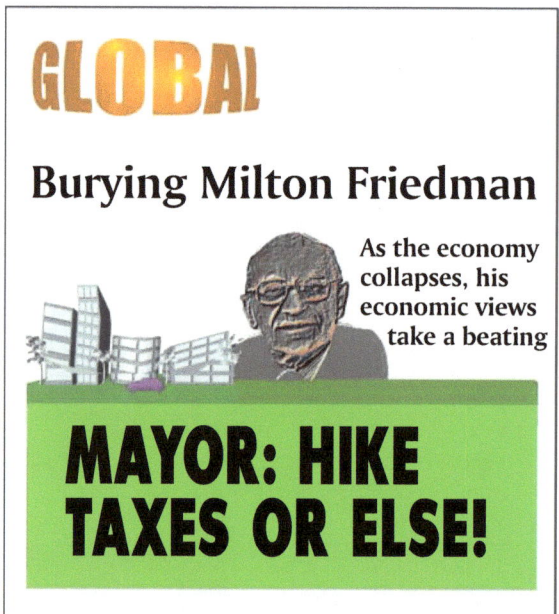

This is a layout for a magazine cover or a tabloid newspaper. Using a large photo or graphic of a person and a small one of a scene can be very effective. (See page 113.)

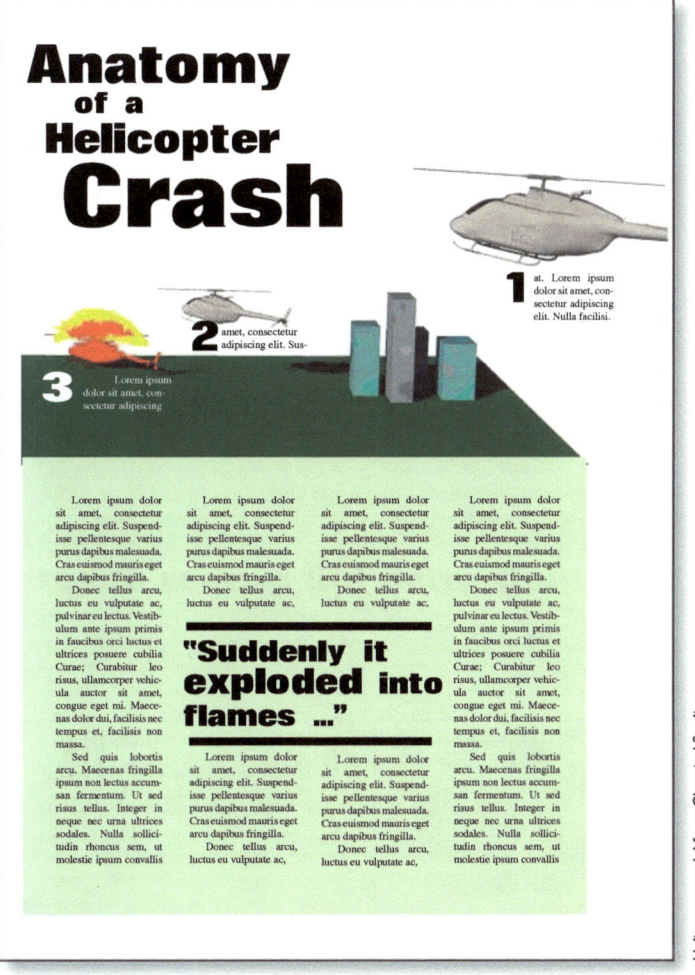

Helicopter model from Chemical Studios

*A large news graphic shows the stages involved in a helicopter crash The text holder in front must be a light color if the body type is to be legible.*

# 3D IN PRINT

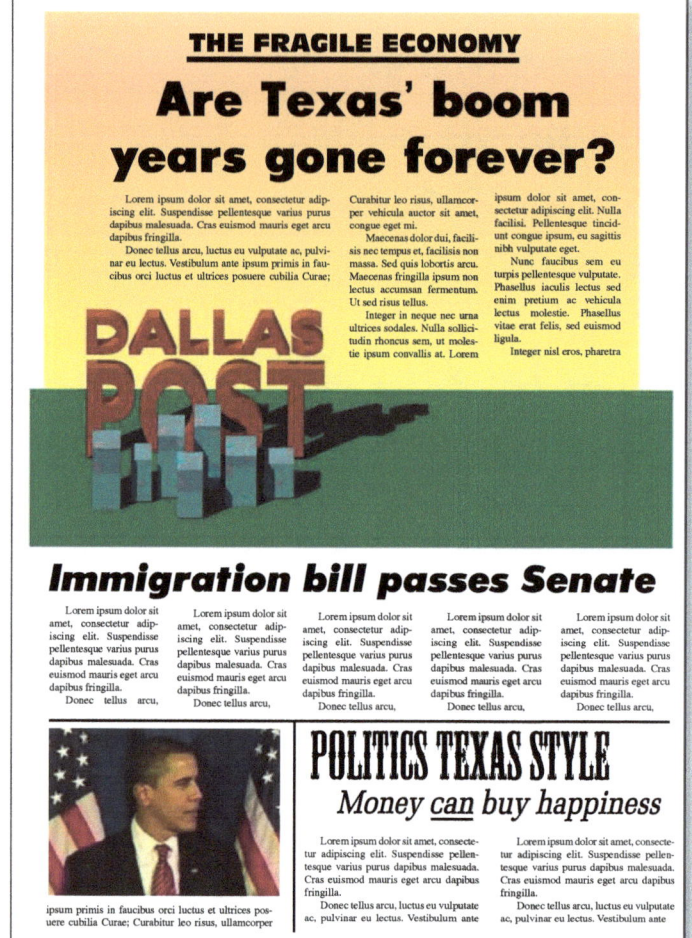

The newspaper logo is part of the artwork. The body type for the story at the top is obviously part of the background. This is an example of a layout set up quickly and roughly in a 3D application.

# 3D IN PRINT

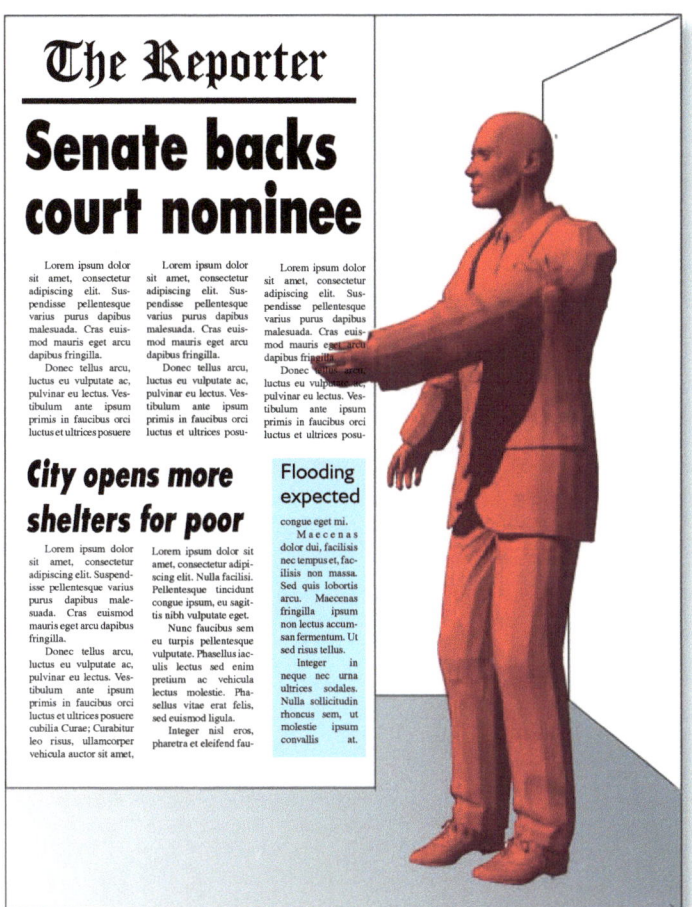

*Sometimes you need to challenge old ideas and try new ones. Here, the newspaper page becomes part of a 3D scene. A 3D model or photo of the court nominee could be substituted for the model shown above.*

# Using a 3D Box

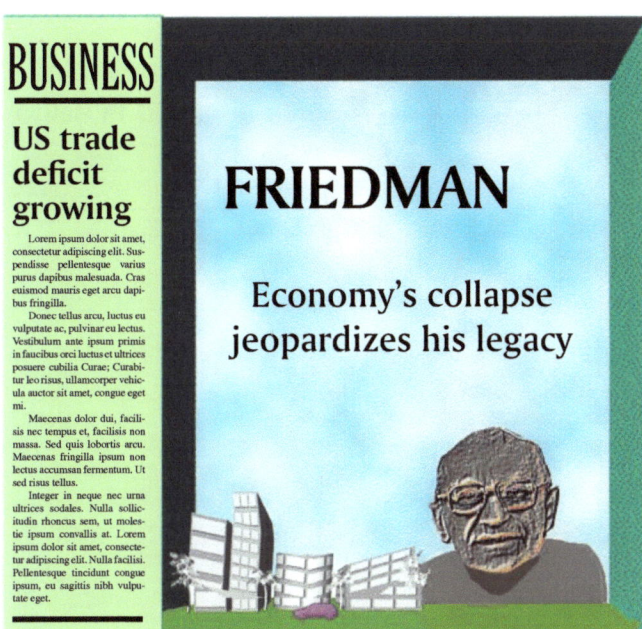

***Without the box and the 3D graphic, this would be just another page.***

# 3D IN PRINT

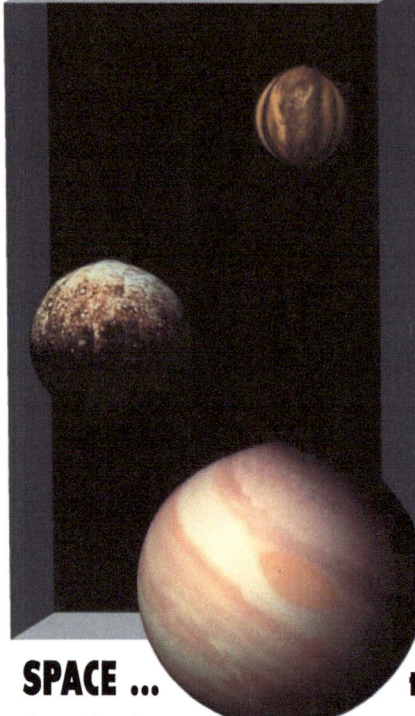

*The 3D box is an effective way of simulating depth on a page. The "comin' at you" effect of the planets also helps. Who needs 3D glasses?*

# 3D IN PRINT

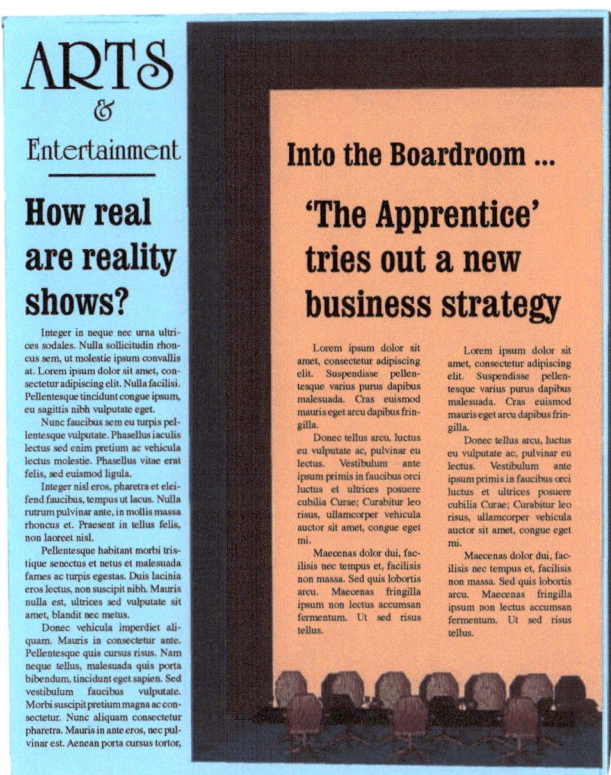

*The 3D box seems to be carved out of the page.*

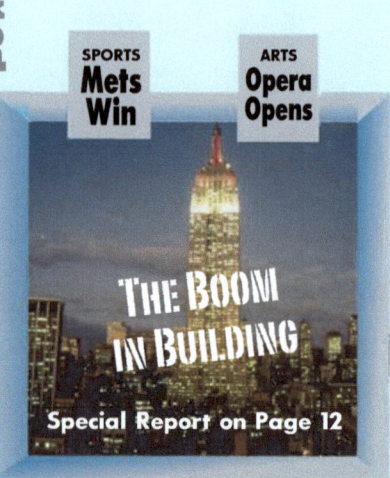

*The box was set up in a 3D program.*
*Art and type were added later.*

# 3D IN PRINT

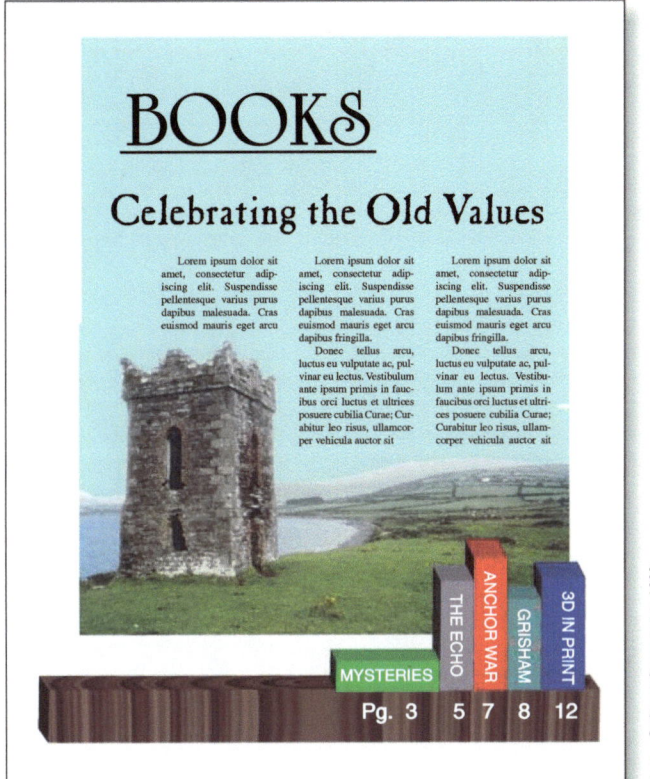

*By adding a shelf and books in front, the layout becomes more interesting. The clear separation between the shelf and the photo emphasizes the 3D effect.*

# Using Photos
# for 3D Effects

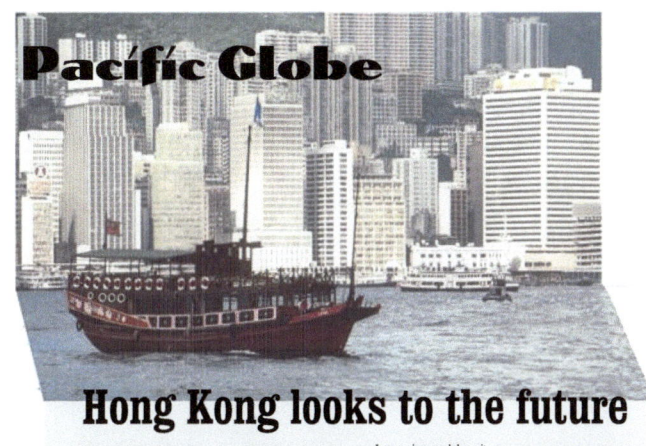

*Creative cropping of the photo gives this page its 3D effect. Type is arranged to emphasize the effect.*

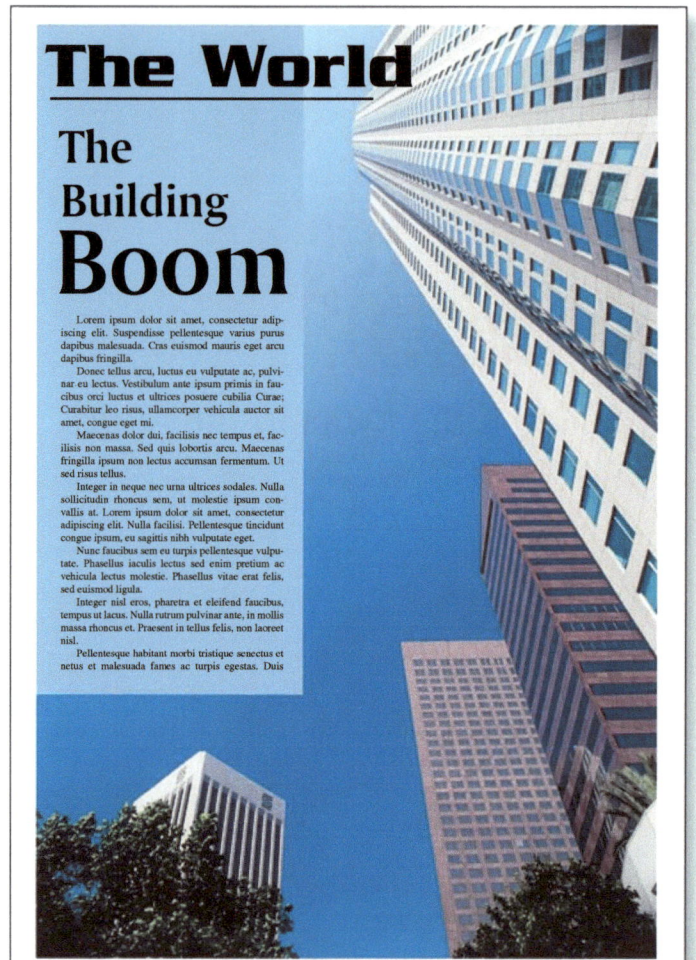

*Photo: © Corel Corporation 1993*

*IMPACT! Some photos have a great natural 3D aspect. Playing them big adds to the effect.*

# 3D IN PRINT

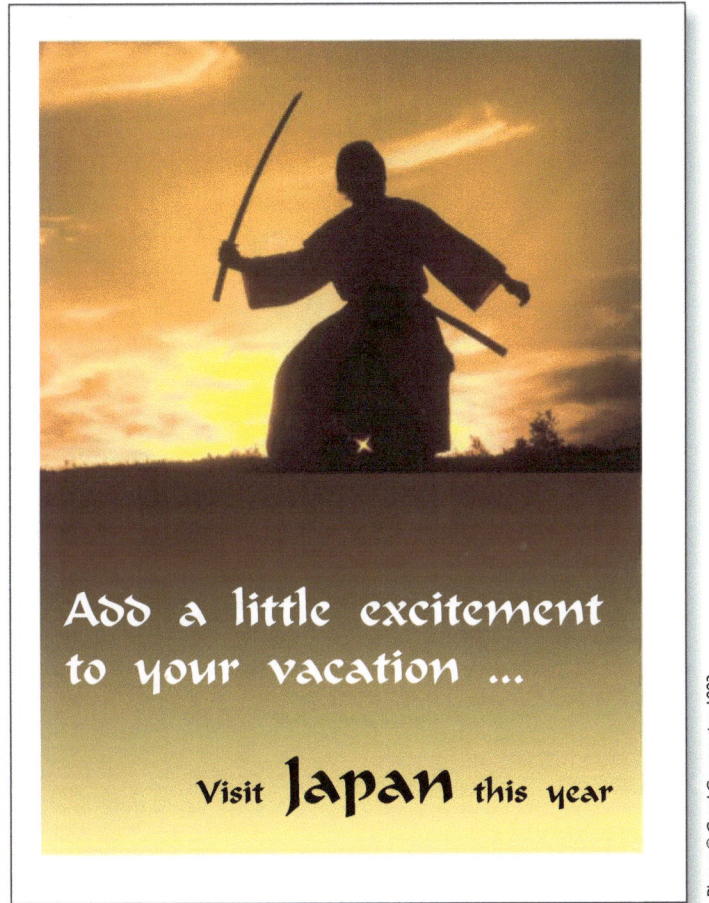

Photo: © Corel Corporation 1993

*The photo dominates the layout and brings it alive.*

# 3D IN PRINT

Lorem ipsum dolor sit amet, consectetur adipiscing elit. Suspendisse pellentesque varius purus dapibus malesuada. Cras euismod mauris eget arcu dapibus fringilla.

Donec tellus arcu, luctus eu vulputate ac, pulvinar eu lectus. Vestibulum ante ipsum primis in faucibus orci luctus et ultrices posuere cubilia Curae; Curabitur leo risus, ullamcorper vehicula auctor sit amet, congue eget mi.

Maecenas dolor dui, facilisis nec tempus et, facilisis non massa. Sed quis lobortis arcu. Maecenas fringilla ipsum non lectus accumsan fermentum. Ut sed risus tellus.

Integer in neque nec urna ultrices sodales. Nulla sollicitudin rhoncus sem, ut molestie ipsum convallis at. Lorem ipsum dolor sit amet, consectetur adipiscing elit. Nulla facilisi. Pellentesque tincidunt congue ipsum, eu sagittis nibh vulputate eget.

Nunc faucibus sem eu turpis pellentesque vulputate. Phasellus iaculis lectus sed enim pretium ac vehicula lectus molestie. Phasellus vitae erat felis, sed euismod ligula.

*Don't just read about the zoo . . . Experience it!*

A "comin' at you" approach for a photo of an elephant. The limitations imposed by two dimensions and columns of type are shattered.

# 3D IN PRINT

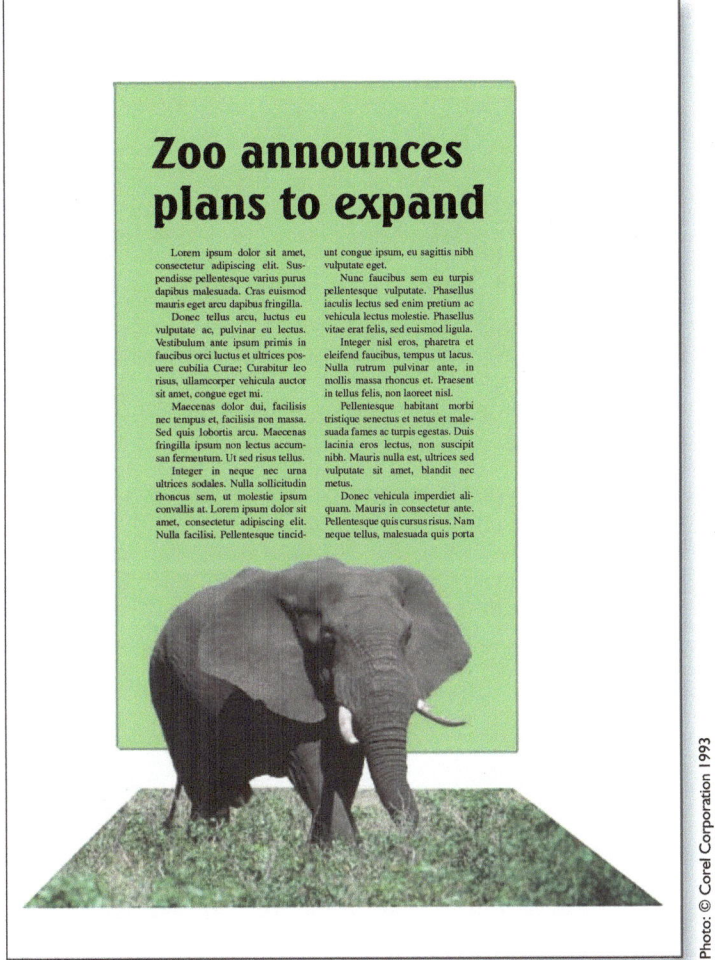

*The same elephant photo is given a different cropping.*

# 3D IN PRINT

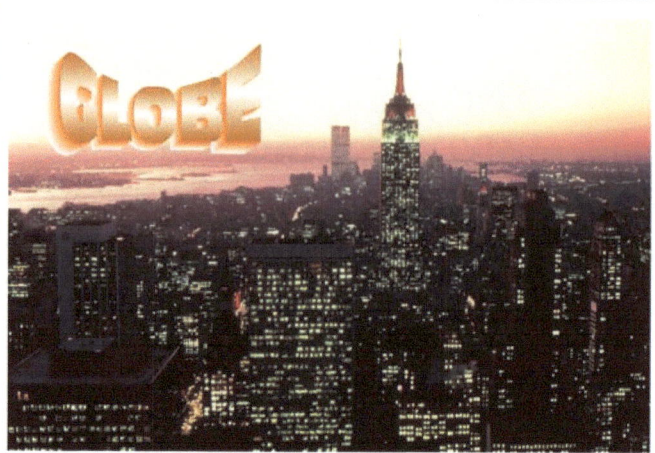

*3D type incorporated into a photograph.*

# 3D IN PRINT

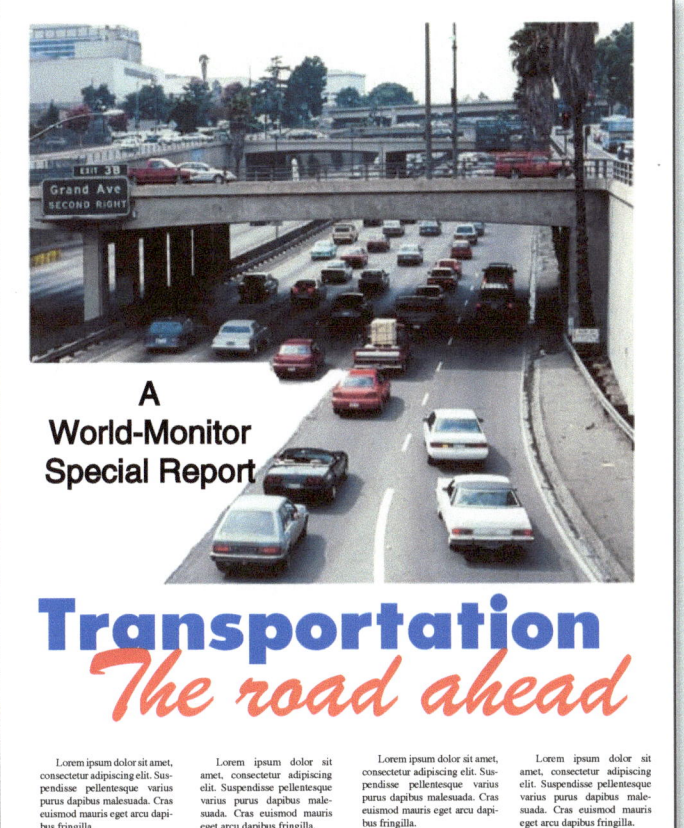

*Photo: © Corel Corporation 1993*

**Cropping emphasizes the "comin' at you" 3D effect.**

# 3D Effects With Type

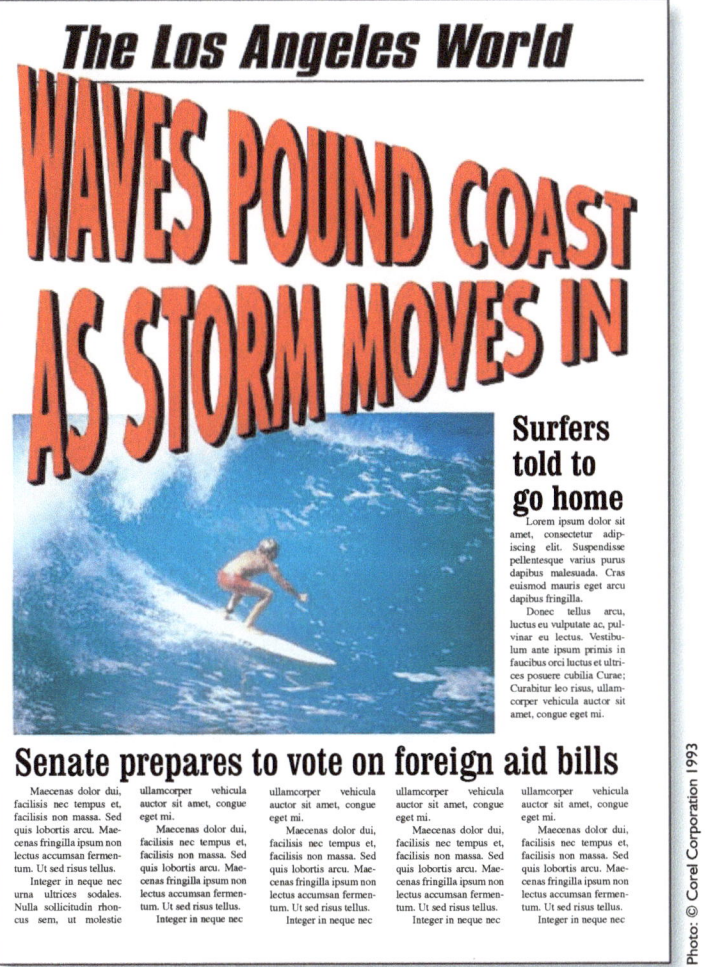

The zoom head leaps off the page. This one was created in TypeStyler.

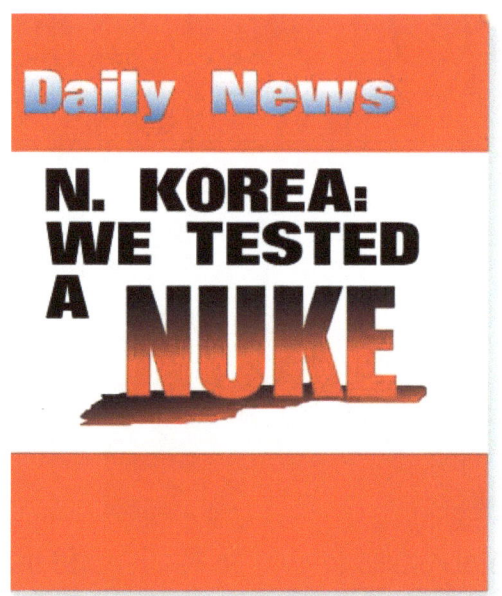

*A simple but effective layout*

# 3D IN PRINT

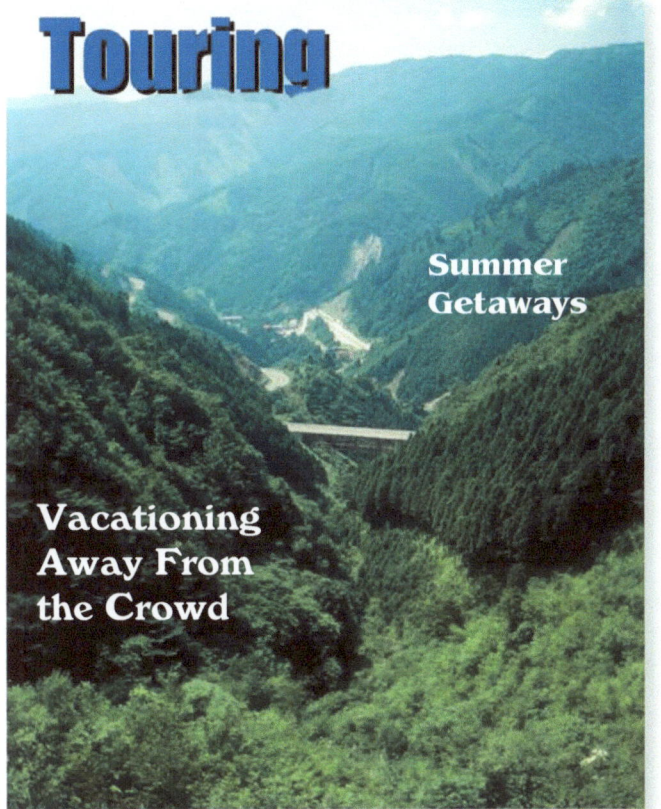

Photo: © Corel Corporation 1993

*The natural 3D perspective of the photo and the sizes of the headline type are keys to this layout.*

# 3D IN PRINT

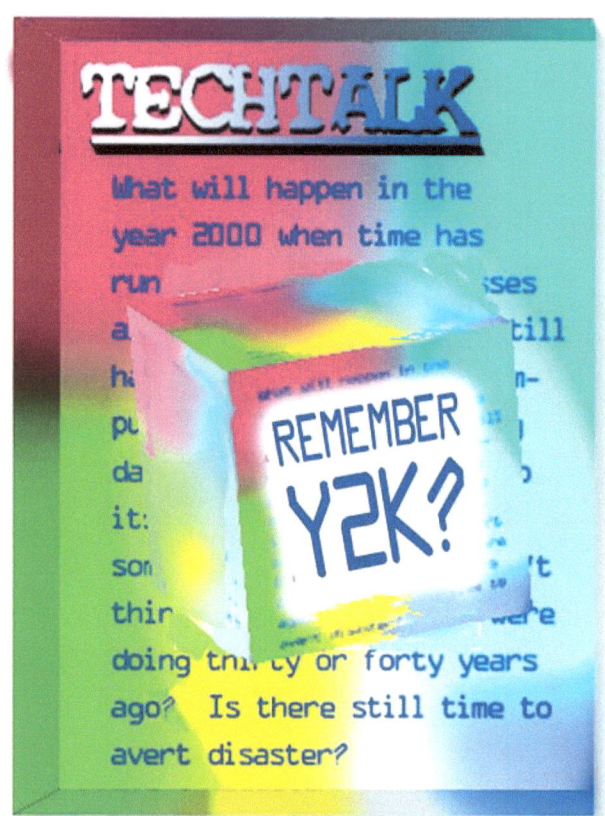

*A 3D box and a 3D graphic dress up this magazine cover.*

# 3D IN PRINT

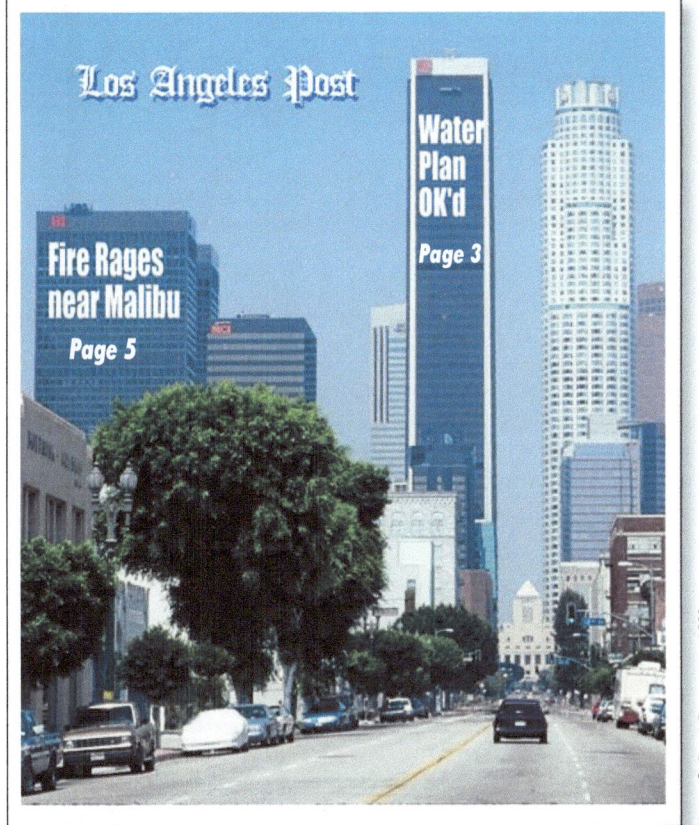

Photo: © Corel Corporation 1993

*An unusual way of reporting the news that brings it into the real world.*

# More Newspaper Pages

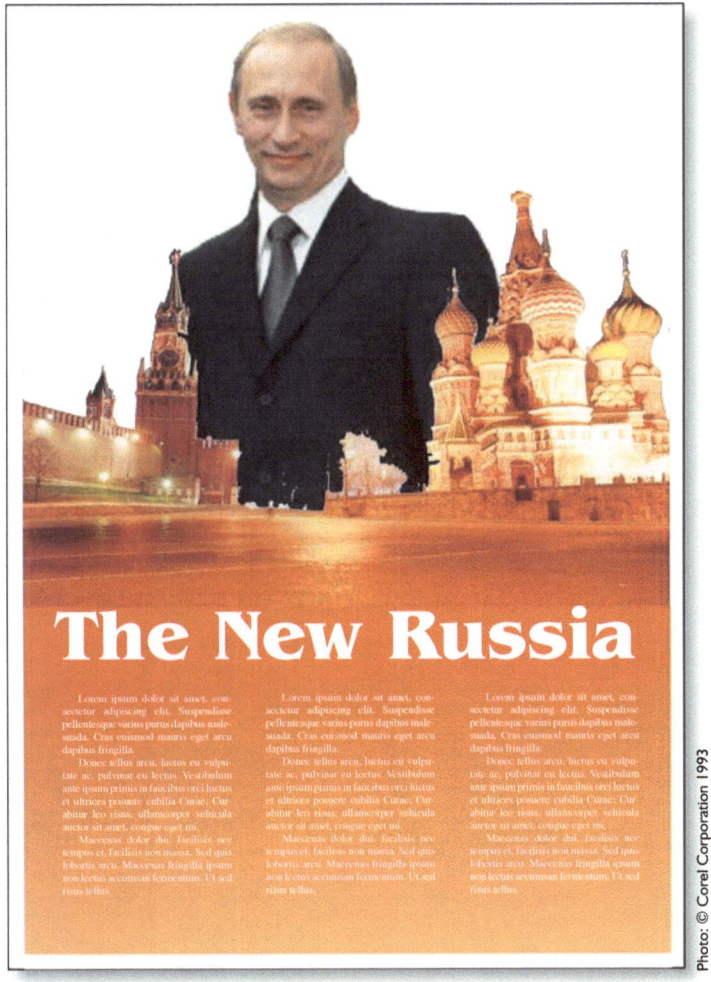

Photo: © Corel Corporation 1993

*Two photographs are used in a way that enriches the news coverage.*

# 3D IN PRINT

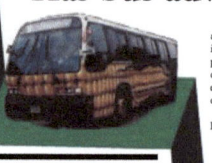

## Opinion

# Has bus advertising gone too far?

Lorem ipsum dolor sit amet, consectetur adipiscing elit. Suspendisse pellentesque varius purus dapibus malesuada. Cras euismod mauris eget arcu dapibus fringilla.

Donec tellus arcu, luctus eu vulputate ac,

Lorem ipsum dolor sit amet, consectetur adipiscing elit. Suspendisse pellentesque varius purus dapibus malesuada. Cras euismod mauris eget arcu dapibus fringilla.

Donec tellus arcu, luctus eu vulputate ac,

Lorem ipsum dolor sit amet, consectetur adipiscing elit. Suspendisse pellentesque varius purus dapibus malesuada. Cras euismod mauris eget arcu dapibus fringilla.

Donec tellus arcu, luctus eu vulputate ac,

## The Press
### Sunday, June 7, 2009

## Property tax cut long overdue

Lorem ipsum dolor sit amet, consectetur adipiscing elit. Suspendisse pellentesque varius purus dapibus malesuada. Cras euismod mauris eget arcu dapibus fringilla.

Donec tellus arcu, luctus eu vulputate ac, pulvinar eu lectus. Vestibulum ante ipsum primis in faucibus orci luctus et ultrices posuere cubilia Curae; Curabitur leo risus, ullamcorper vehicula auctor sit amet, congue eget mi.

Maecenas dolor dui, facilisis nec tempus et, facilisis non massa. Sed quis lobortis arcu. Maecenas fringilla ipsum non lectus accumsan fermentum. Ut sed risus tellus.

Integer in neque nec urna ultrices sodales. Nulla sollicitudin rhoncus sem, ut molestie ipsum convallis at. Lorem ipsum dolor sit amet, consectetur adipiscing elit. Nulla facilisi. Pellentesque tincidunt congue ipsum, eu sagittis nibh vulputate eget.

Nunc faucibus sem eu turpis pellen-

## Bring the troops home

tesque vulputate. Phasellus iaculis lectus sed enim pretium ac vehicula lectus molestie. Phasellus vitae erat felis, sed euismod ligula.

Integer nisl eros, pharetra et eleifend faucibus, tempus ut lacus. Nulla rutrum pulvinar ante, in mollis massa rhoncus et. Praesent in tellus felis, non laoreet nisl.

Pellentesque habitant morbi tristique senectus et netus et malesuada fames ac turpis egestas. Duis lacinia eros lectus, non suscipit nibh. Mauris nulla est, ultrices sed vulputate sit amet, blandit nec metus.

Donec vehicula imperdiet aliquam. Mauris in consectetur ante. Pellentesque quis cursus risus. Nam neque tellus, malesuada quis porta bibendum, tincidunt eget sapien. Sed vestibulum faucibus vulpu-

## The Freelance

# Republican candidates targeting liberal 'threat' in ad campaigns

Lorem ipsum dolor sit amet, consectetur adipiscing elit. Suspendisse pellentesque varius purus dapibus malesuada. Cras euismod mauris eget arcu dapibus fringilla.

Donec tellus arcu, luctus eu vulputate ac, pulvinar eu lectus. Vestibulum ante ipsum primis in faucibus orci luctus et ultrices posuere cubilia Curae; Curabitur leo risus, ullamcorper vehicula auctor sit amet, congue eget mi.

Maecenas dolor dui, fac-

Lorem ipsum dolor sit amet, consectetur adipiscing elit. Suspendisse pellentesque varius purus dapibus malesuada. Cras euismod mauris eget arcu dapibus fringilla.

Donec tellus arcu, luctus eu vulputate ac, pulvinar eu lectus. Vestibulum ante ipsum primis in faucibus orci luctus et ultrices posuere cubilia Curae; Curabitur leo risus, ullamcorper vehicula auctor sit amet, congue eget mi.

Maecenas dolor dui, fac

Lorem ipsum dolor sit amet, consectetur adipiscing elit. Suspendisse pellentesque varius purus dapibus malesuada. Cras euismod mauris eget arcu dapibus fringilla.

Donec tellus arcu, luctus eu vulputate ac, pulvinar eu lectus. Vestibulum ante ipsum primis in faucibus orci luctus et ultrices posuere cubilia Curae; Curabitur leo risus, ullamcorper vehicula auctor sit amet, congue eget mi.

Maecenas dolor dui, fac

# Congressmen obey their own law

ilisis nec tempus et, facilisis non massa. Sed quis lobortis arcu. Maecenas fringilla ipsum non lectus accumsan fermentum. Ut sed risus tellus.

Integer in neque nec urna ultrices sodales. Nulla sollicitudin rhoncus sem, ut molestie ipsum convallis at. Lorem ipsum dolor sit amet, consectetur adipiscing elit. Nulla facilisi. Pellentesque tincidunt congue ipsum, eu sagittis nibh vulputate eget.

ilisis nec tempus et, facilisis non massa. Sed quis lobortis arcu. Maecenas fringilla ipsum non lectus accumsan fermentum. Ut sed risus tellus.

Integer in neque nec urna ultrices sodales. Nulla sollicitudin rhoncus sem, ut molestie ipsum convallis at. Lorem ipsum dolor sit amet, consectetur adipiscing elit. Nulla facilisi. Pellentesque tincidunt congue ipsum, eu sagittis nibh vulputate

ilisis nec tempus et, facilisis non massa. Sed quis lobortis arcu. Maecenas fringilla ipsum non lectus accumsan fermentum. Ut sed risus tellus.

Integer in neque nec urna ultrices sodales. Nulla sollicitudin rhoncus sem, ut molestie ipsum convallis at. Lorem ipsum dolor sit amet, consectetur adipiscing elit. Nulla facilisi. Pellentesque tincidunt congue ipsum, eu sagittis nibh vulputate

*A variation of the "3D shelf" idea. Even editorial pages can be dressed up with 3D layouts.*

# Magazine Pages

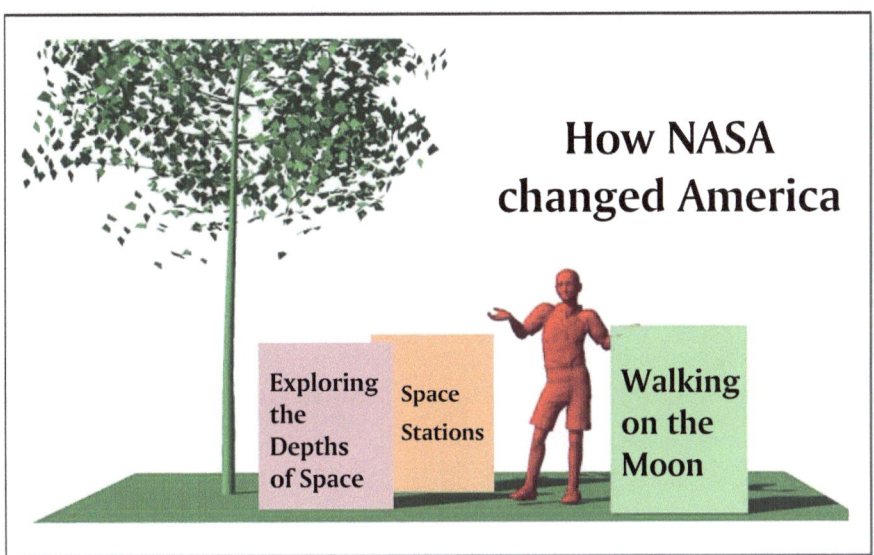

*Type is incorporated into a 3D scene.*

# 3D IN PRINT

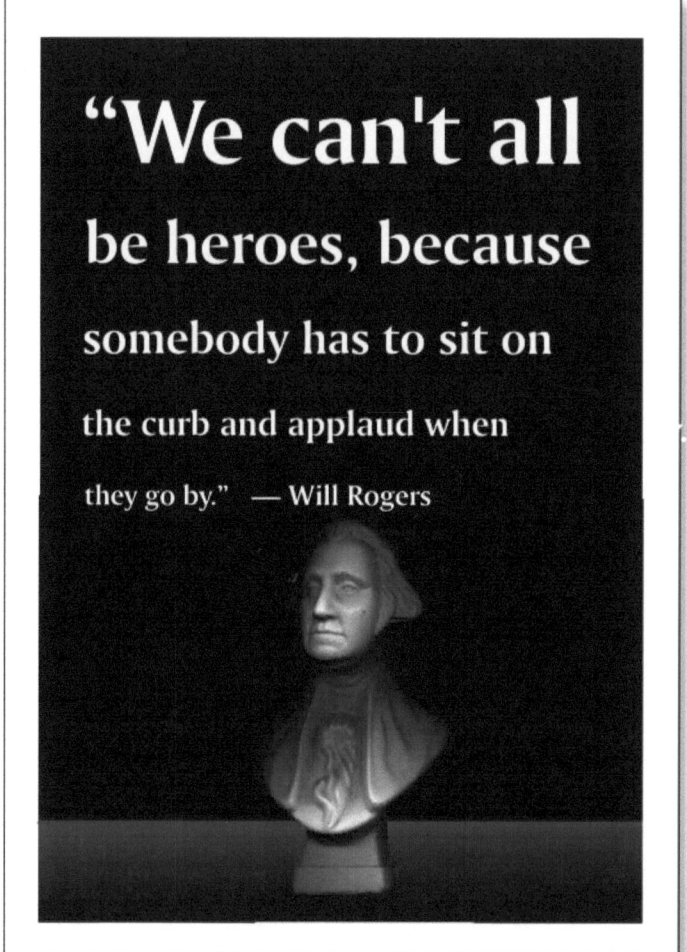

"We can't all be heroes, because somebody has to sit on the curb and applaud when they go by." — Will Rogers

*The bust of Washington adds depth to the page.*

# 3D IN PRINT

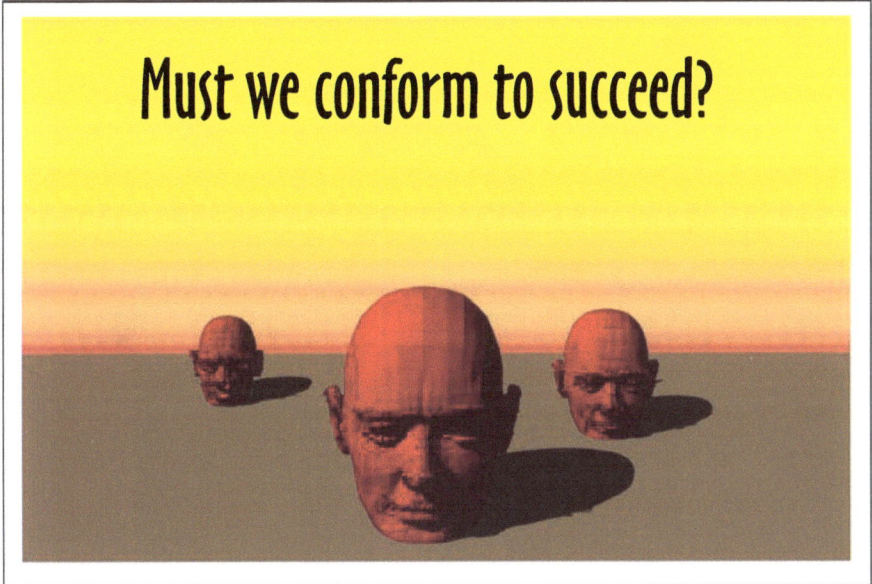

*Shadows and depth make this magazine-type spread effective.*

# 3D IN PRINT

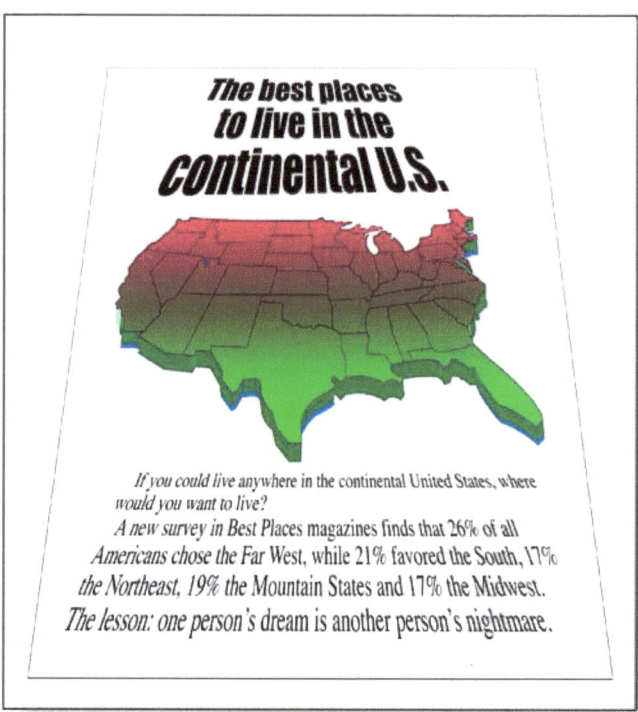

*Lines around the graphic emphasize the 3D perspective. The graphic and type were manipulated in Photoshop.*

# 3D IN PRINT

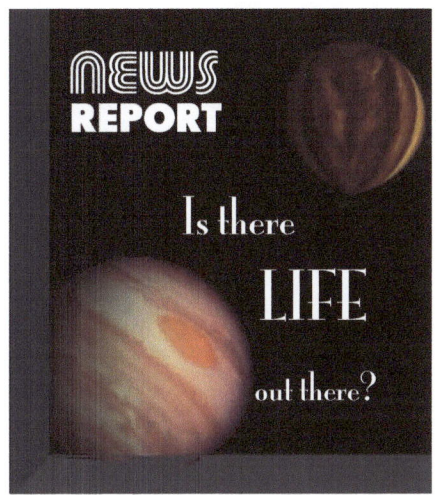

This magazine cover uses the 3D box
design.

# Advertisements

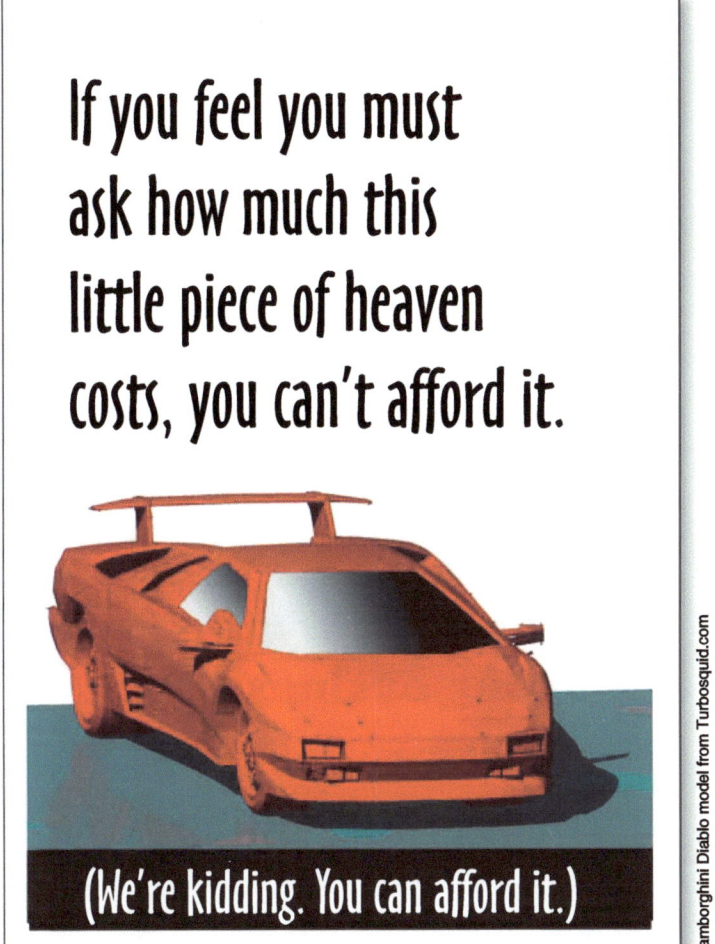

If you feel you must
ask how much this
little piece of heaven
costs, you can't afford it.

(We're kidding. You can afford it.)

Lamborghini Diablo model from Turbosquid.com

*A different approach to the "comin' at you" idea.*

# 3D IN PRINT

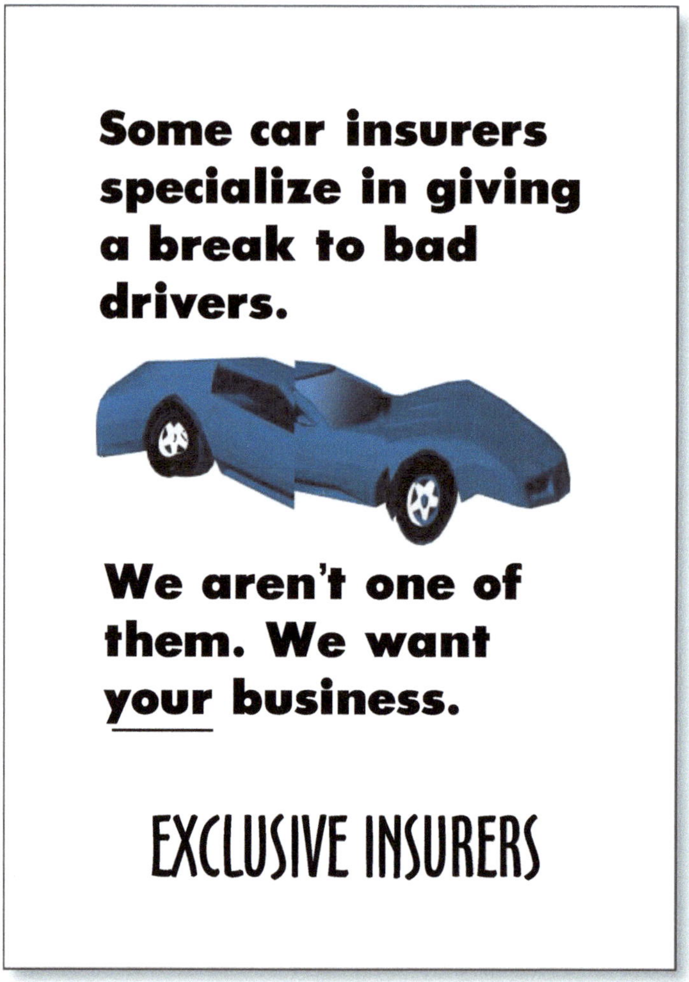
Some car insurers specialize in giving a break to bad drivers.
We aren't one of them. We want your business.
EXCLUSIVE INSURERS

Corvette model from Turbosquid.com

*A 3D filter in Photoshop wrecked this car.*

# 3D IN PRINT

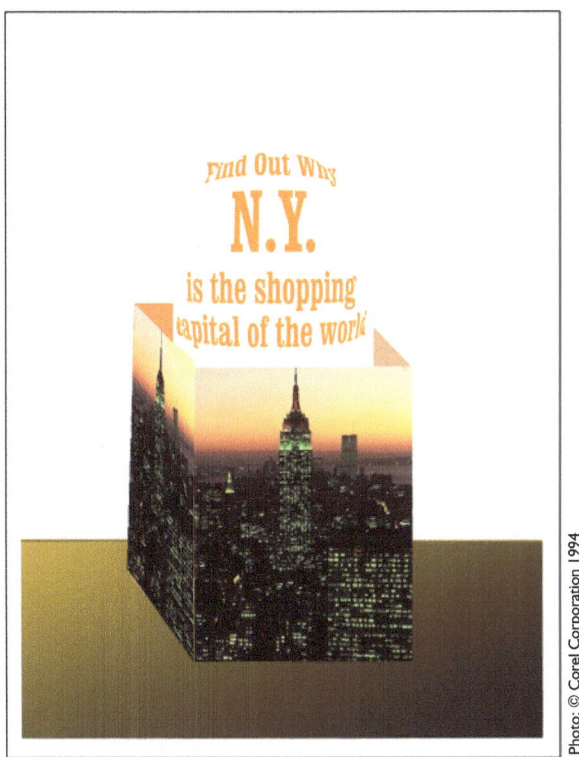

Photo: © Corel Corporation 1994

The "shopping bag" could be created in a 3D application or in graphics software such as Adobe Photoshop.

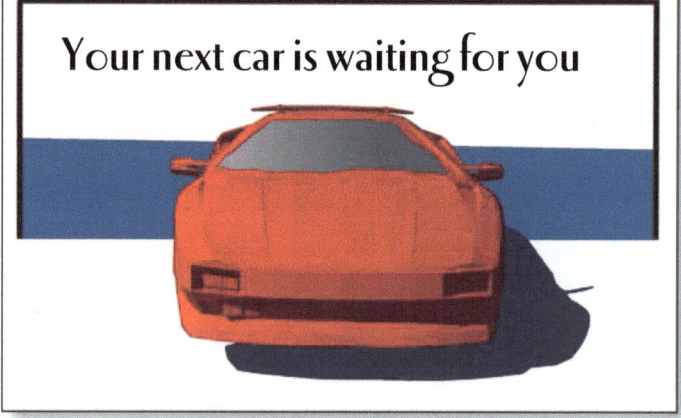

# Storm pounds coast

Lorem ipsum dolor sit amet, consectetur adipiscing elit. Suspendisse pellentesque varius purus dapibus malesuada. Cras euismod mauris eget arcu dapibus fringilla.

Donec tellus arcu, luctus eu vulputate ac, pulvinar eu lectus. Vestibulum ante ipsum primis in faucibus orci luctus et ultrices posuere cubilia Curae; Curabitur leo risus, ullamcorper vehicula auctor sit amet, congue eget mi.

Maecenas dolor dui, facilisis nec tempus et, facilisis non massa. Sed quis lobortis arcu. Maecenas fringilla ipsum non lectus accumsan fermentum. Ut sed risus tellus.

Integer in neque nec urna ultrices sodales. Nulla sollicitudin rhoncus sem, ut molestie ipsum convallis at. Lorem ipsum dolor sit amet, consectetur adipiscing elit. Nulla facilisi. Pellentesque tincidunt congue ipsum, eu sagittis nibh vulputate eget.

Lorem ipsum dolor sit amet, consectetur adipiscing elit. Suspendisse pellentesque varius purus dapibus malesuada. Cras euismod mauris eget arcu dapibus fringilla.

Donec tellus arcu, luctus eu vulputate ac, pulvinar eu lectus. Vestibulum ante ipsum primis in faucibus orci luctus et ultrices posuere cubilia Curae; Curabitur leo risus,

## Power outages leave 200,000 Philadelphians in the dark

ullamcorper vehicula auctor sit amet, congue eget mi.

Maecenas dolor dui, facilisis nec tempus et, facilisis non massa. Sed quis lobortis arcu. Maecenas fringilla ipsum non lectus accumsan fermentum. Ut sed risus tellus.

Integer in neque nec urna ultrices sodales. Nulla sollicitudin rhoncus sem, ut moles-

Lorem ipsum dolor sit amet, consectetur adipiscing elit. Suspendisse pellentesque varius purus dapibus malesuada. Cras euismod mauris eget arcu dapibus fringilla.

Donec tellus arcu, luctus eu vulputate ac, pulvinar eu lectus. Vestibulum ante ipsum primis in faucibus orci luctus et ultrices posuere cubilia Curae; Curabitur leo risus,

ullamcorper vehicula auctor sit amet, congue eget mi.

Maecenas dolor dui, facilisis nec tempus et, facilisis non massa. Sed quis lobortis arcu. Maecenas fringilla ipsum non lectus accumsan fermentum. Ut sed risus tellus.

Integer in neque nec urna ultrices sodales. Nulla sollicitudin rhoncus sem, ut moles-

Lorem ipsum dolor sit amet, consectetur adipiscing elit. Suspendisse pellentesque varius purus dapibus malesuada. Cras euismod mauris eget arcu dapibus fringilla.

Donec tellus arcu, luctus eu vulputate ac, pulvinar eu lectus. Vestibulum ante ipsum primis in faucibus orci luctus et ultrices posuere cubilia Curae; Curabitur leo risus, ullamcorper vehicula auctor sit amet, congue eget mi.

Maecenas dolor dui, facilisis nec tempus et, facilisis non massa. Sed quis lobortis arcu. Maecenas fringilla ipsum non lectus accumsan fermentum. Ut sed risus tellus.

Integer in neque nec urna ultrices sodales. Nulla sollicitudin rhoncus sem, ut molestie ipsum convallis at. Lorem ipsum dolor sit amet, consectetur adipiscing elit. Nulla facilisi. Pellentesque tincidunt congue ipsum, eu sagittis nibh vulputate eget.

## Your next car is waiting for you

Lamborghini Diablo model from Turbosquid.com

*The partial border around the ad emphasizes the "comin' at you" idea. The page also is effective because the editorial layout is simple and attractive.*

# 3D IN PRINT

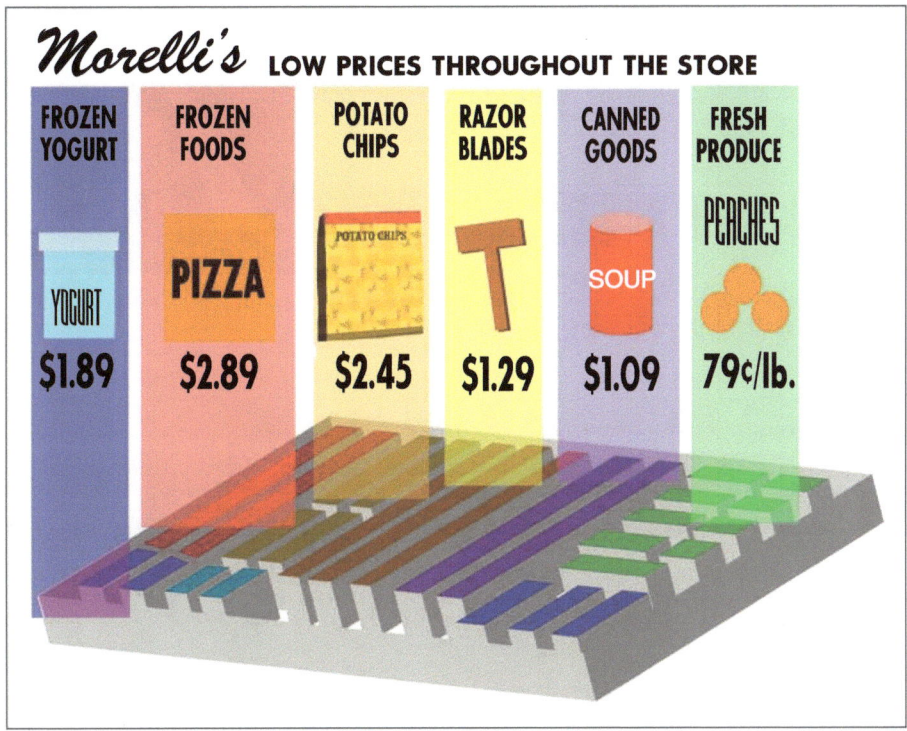

*This design for a grocery ad would be suitable for a flyer or newspaper insert. The 3D model illustrates a layout of the store. The sale items are shown in relation to their location.*

# 3D IN PRINT

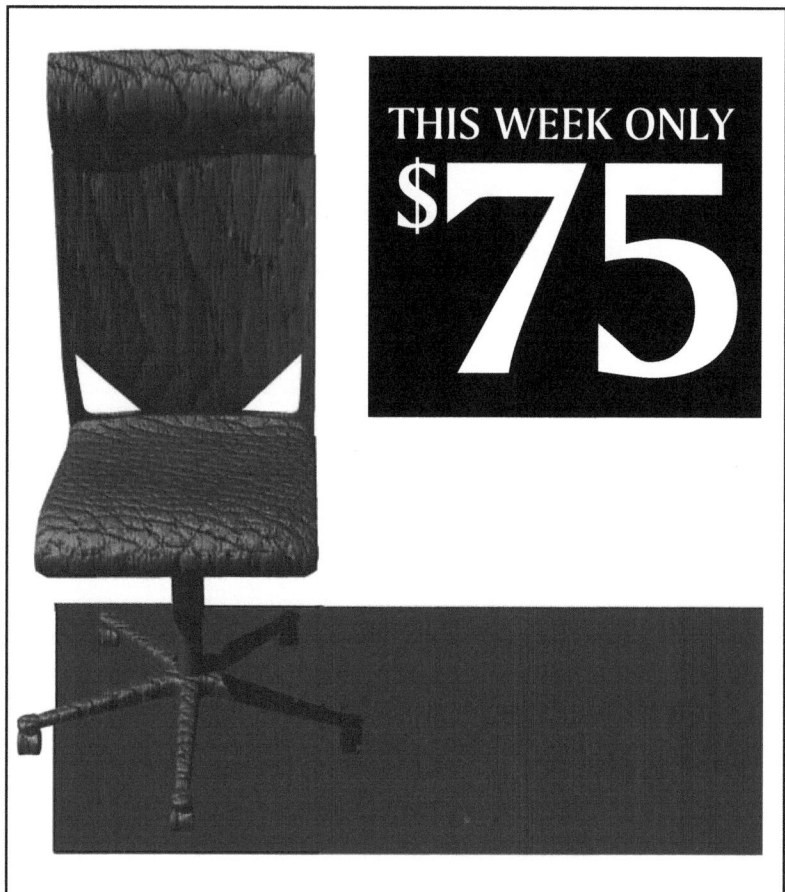

THIS WEEK ONLY
$75

*The 3D model of the chair gives this page more impact.*

# Other Media

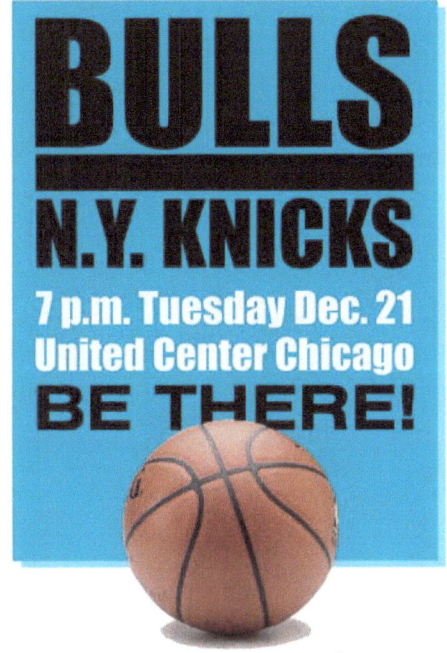

Basketball photo © CMCD 1994

*The type is big and bold, but it's the basketball that give this poster impact and a 3D effect.*

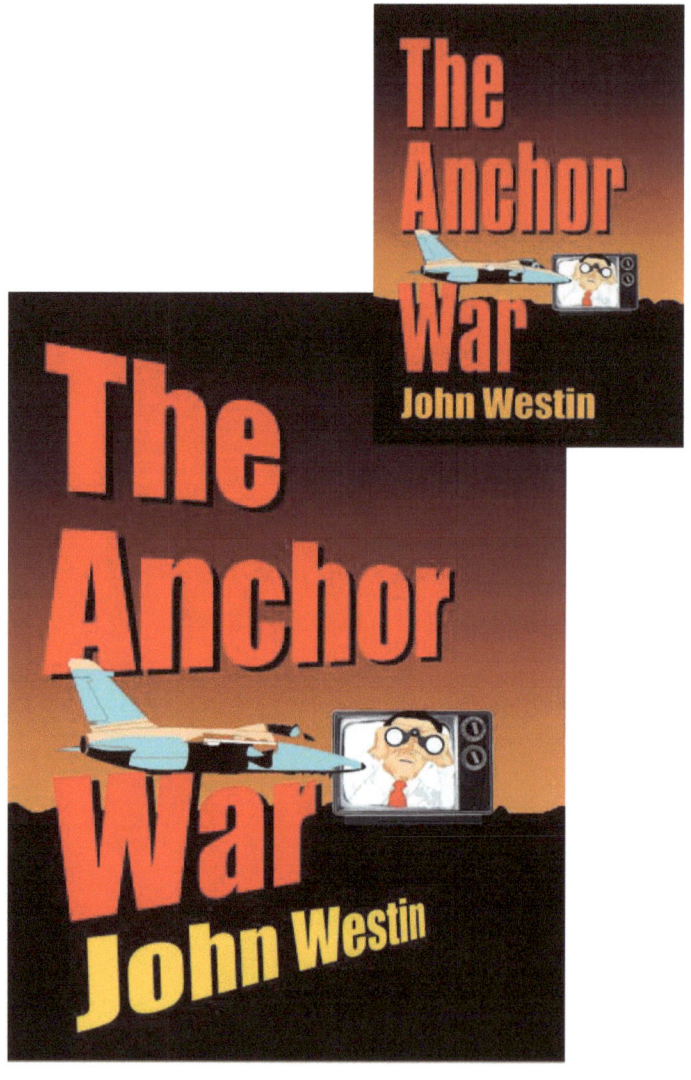

*Perspective type would have given the book cover shown at upper right more of a 3D feeling.*

# 3D IN PRINT

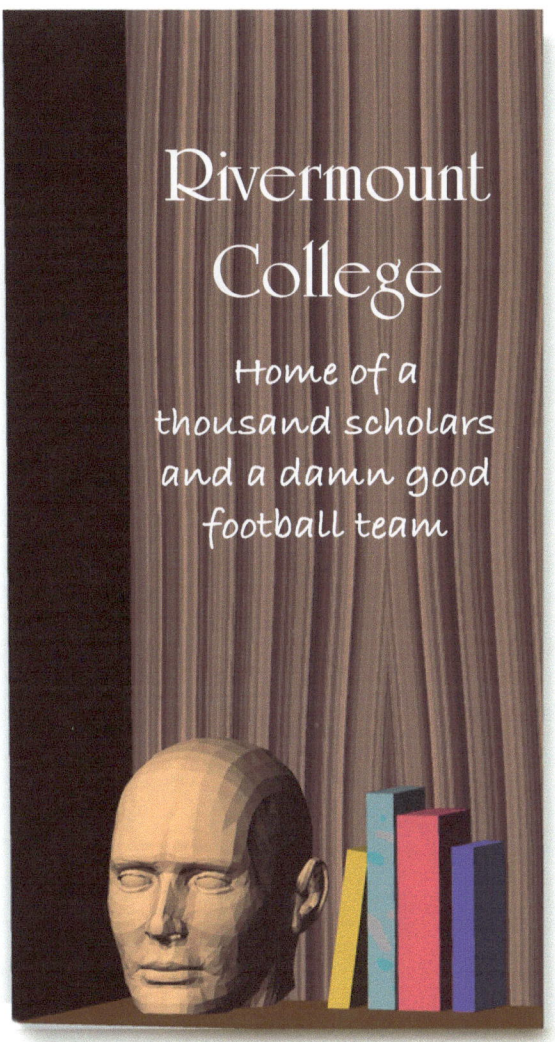

Rivermount
College

Home of a
thousand scholars
and a damn good
football team

Design for a college brochure. The 3D
box takes the form of a wood cabinet.
The books could be mapped with the
covers of real books.

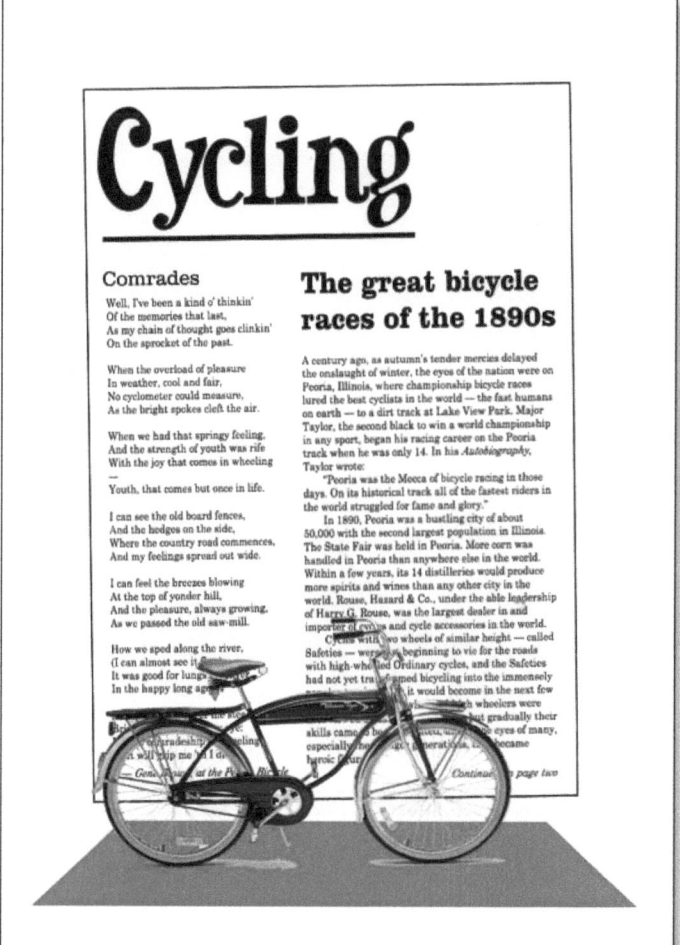

Bicycle photo © CMCD 1994

*The newsletter and the photo of the bicycle were combined in Photoshop.*

## What have they done to my home?

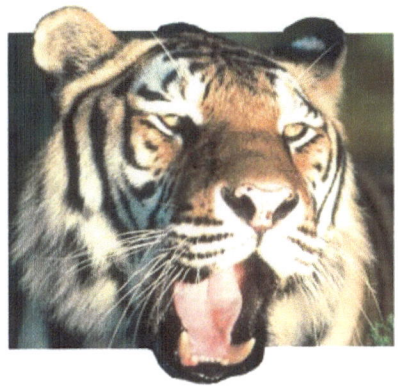

## Come see for yourself!

# The Metroplex Zoo

Photo © Corel Corporation 1993

*Creative cropping makes the tiger more menacing.*

# 3D IN PRINT

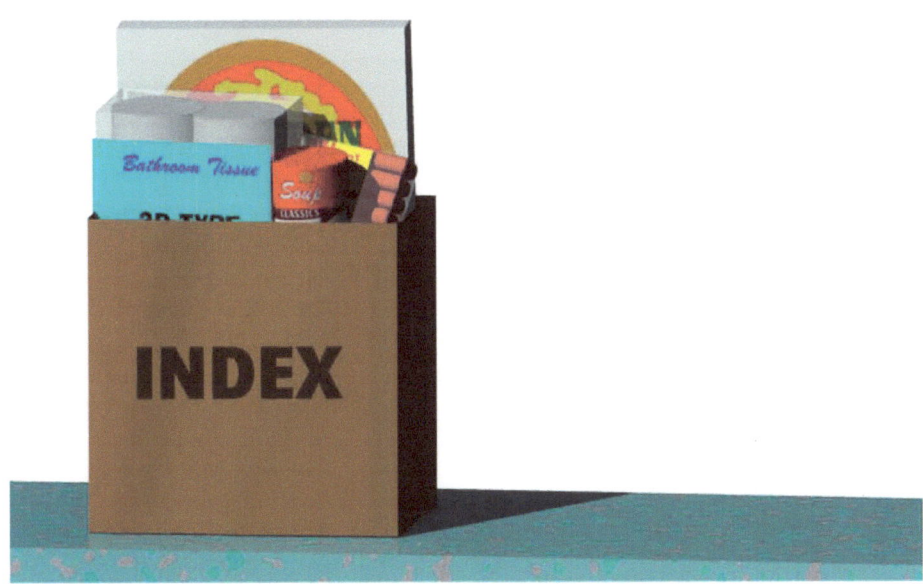

# 3D IN PRINT

# 3D IN PRINT

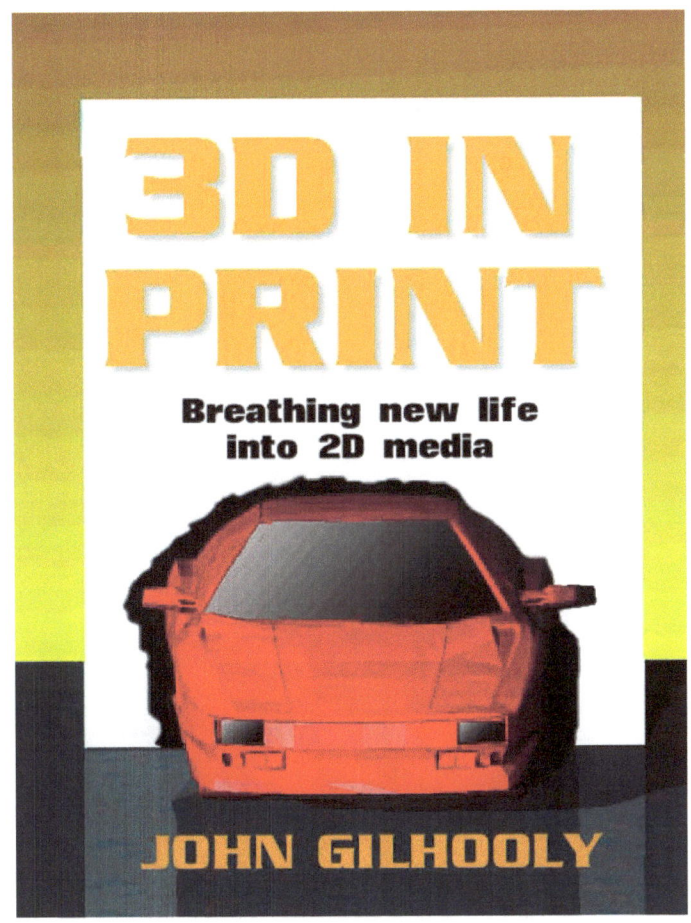

THREE TV REPORTERS BATTLE
FOR A NETWORK ANCHOR
JOB AS THE 1991 WAR
ON IRAQ BEGINS

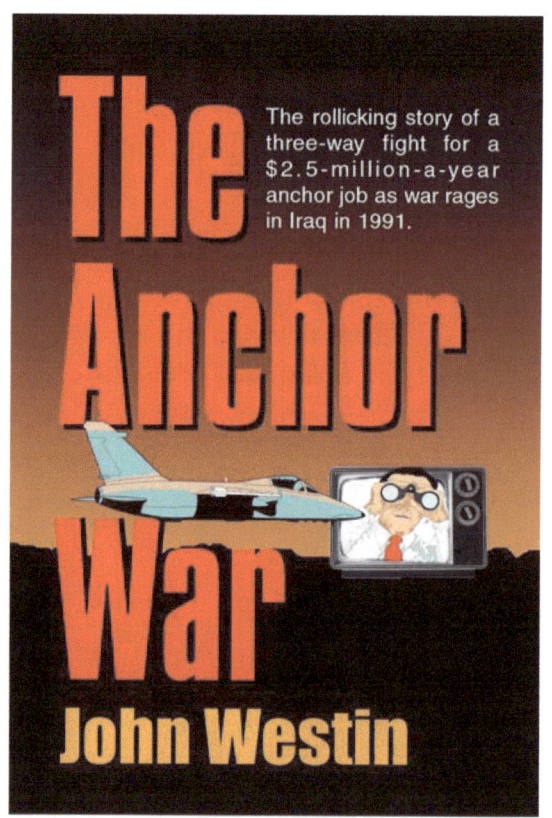

The rollicking story of a three-way fight for a $2.5-million-a-year anchor job as war rages in Iraq in 1991.

The Anchor War

John Westin

AVAILABLE NOW AT AMAZON.COM

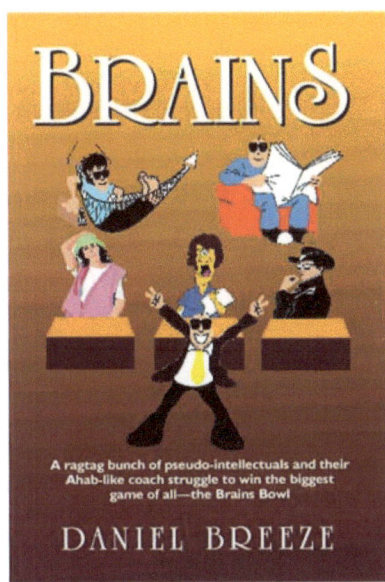

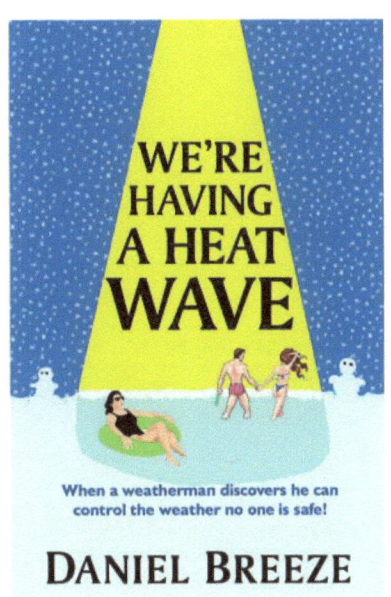

# The Best in Entertaining and Suspenseful Fiction

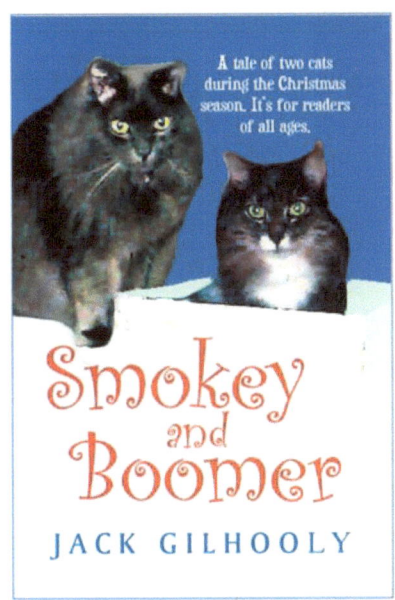

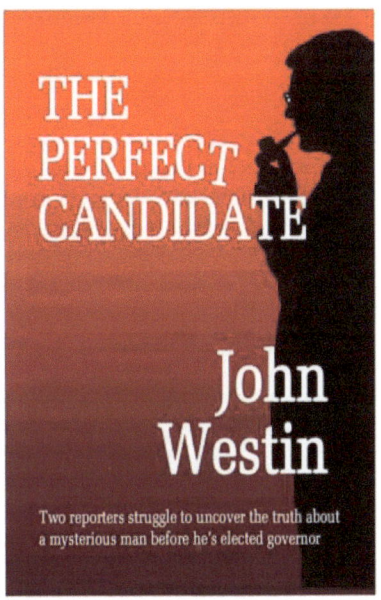

For availability see Amazon.com

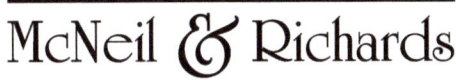

www.ingramcontent.com/pod-product-compliance
Lightning Source LLC
Chambersburg PA
CBHW050716180526
45159CB00003B/1040